## Praise for *Horse Sense, Business Sense* and S

*"Until you start to dig around, a new equine facilitated business doesn't necessarily have a place to begin. This book will be the new start-up Bible for my development as an equine practitioner and entrepreneur. I've had quite a bit put into perspective for me, and you've got me all determined and thoughtful about the possibilities. I am not discouraged; I feel more empowered!"*

Robin Brosmer, *EAGALA Level I*, Orlando FL

*"I wish I'd had something this useful back when S.T.A.R.S. was started. Even now it would be of tremendous help for our board and the instructors to read this. This is a good time in the history of therapeutic riding and psychotherapeutic programs for [this information] to be presented. I think the industry will be thankful to have such a thorough resource available."*

Sue Wheeler, Founder, *S.T.A.R.S. Program*, Iowa

*"Thanks for being the dedicated individual you are and 'taking the time it takes' to educate the rest of us so that this growing discipline can be something that will significantly impact horses and people in a positive way."*

Lisa Martin, *Kingdom Equus Equine Assisted Programs*, Alabama

*"Shannon is very accommodating and shows an honest interest in helping this business . . . she is eager to share the work she has done to save others time and frustration."*

Vikki J. Pease, *Horses Helping Humans*, SC

*"I would say if you are interested in starting your own EAP/EAL business and need advice . . . she is the best.*

Tracy P. Setzler, MPH, MSW, *Family Connection of South Carolina*

*"Many times I feel like this colt, young and inexperienced in my equine business. I thank God for people like [Shannon] willing to help others on their journey."*

Meloney Nunez, *Healing Reigns*, Arizona

# horse sense
## business sense

HINTS AND HURDLES TO STARTING YOUR OWN EQUINE ASSISTED PROGRAM

## BOOK 1
## THE EARLY YEARS

by Shannon Knapp
with Brenda Dammann

*Horse Sense, Business Sense*, Volume 2, First Edition

© 2007 by Shannon Knapp, with Brenda Dammann

Cover Design and interior design: Ginger Graziano, www.gingergraziano.com

Cover Photos by Coco

ISBN-13: 978-0-9794041-0-8

ISBN-10: 0-9794041-0-X



10 9 8 7 6 5 4 3 2

# Table of Contents

Chapter One: **In the Beginning** ........................................................... 1

Chapter Two: **Building *Horse Sense*** ................................... 10

Chapter Three: **Building a Business System** .......................... 34

Chapter Four: **Building a Facility** ............................................ 58

Chapter Five: **Building a Team** ................................................ 70

Chapter Six: **Building Awareness** ......................................... 101

Chapter Seven: **Building Clientele** ....................................... 118

Chapter Eight: **What Lies Beyond** ....................................... 131

**Works Cited & Recommended Reading** ............................ 140

# Chapter ONE

# In the **Beginning**

### How do you start a successful business? And how do you keep it successful?

*T*hose are million dollar questions for sure, even more so when that business is a specialized form of work in a burgeoning industry.* Just ask those
who lived through the birth of the Internet or the dot com bubble. There was no
model for what they did, no traditional business formulas applied. So the industry had
to survive a series of spectacular successes and failures.

The advent of Equine Assisted Psychotherapy (EAP) and Equine Assisted Learning
(EAL) in the past decade has borne a quiet revolution of its own. The growing credibility and value of therapeutic work done with horses has opened new possibilities
for the therapeutic community and the people they serve.

But while the value of equine assisted practice and its various modalities
creates new vistas in the therapy world, EAP/EAL programs face a corresponding
challenge of how to operate and structure themselves in the business world.

Depending on who you talk to, you'll either get the hopeful news or the brutal
truth about small businesses: it's tough to be a small business of any sort and stay
afloat. EAP programs get the double-whammy of being both an equine business and a
therapeutic treatment business, both tricky to get off the ground.

Common business wisdom is that equine-related businesses have a failure rate of
somewhere between that of restaurants and TV sitcoms—maybe as high as 90 to 95
percent in the first three years. The dual therapy/equine aspect of EAP businesses
can suffer from many ills: lack of horse knowledge and background, lack of proper
therapeutic platform, lack of business acumen in management, marketing, or finance.
Professionalism is an absolute necessity. Pair that reality with the complex needs,
liabilities, and sensitivities of both equine and therapy components and you have
every reason to be thoroughly and soundly prepared.

At the same time, however, there is also good reason to be excited by the possibilities and potential of equine assisted practice. So ... how can your business avoid the
pitfalls of typical start-ups and make it past those tricky early stages to success? That
becomes the question at hand.

**M**y name is Shannon Knapp. My business is *Horse Sense of the Carolinas, Inc.,* which offers EAP for individual, family and group therapy sessions, and EAL leadership training with workshops geared towards personal and professional growth. We opened our facility in June 2003 near Asheville, NC, and have grown to become one of the most established Equine Assisted Therapy businesses in the country. This book came about as a result of our struggles and experiences over the last few years—the dynamics that led us to starting a business in the equine assisted therapy world, the choices we made in structuring the business, how we became established, and how *Horse Sense* managed to survive its infancy.

Certainly we've had our share of challenges, and a whole laundry list of things we *wish* we had done differently. Somehow, we made it through the gamut of obstacles, choices, mistakes, and systems, to create a structure that works for us. Our evolution continues to this day.

Even before seeing clients, when *Horse Sense* was nothing but a logo and a website, the phone started ringing with calls from other people interested in starting their own equine assisted business. "How did you do this? How did you do that? How did you solve this issue? What do you recommend?" The interesting thing is that a fair amount of phone calls were not about how to do EAP but were about how to run the *business* around EAP: how to handle insurance, billing, hiring, paying therapists, and marketing.

Somewhere during this same time, we also attempted to create a Standard Operating Procedures (SOP) manual for *Horse Sense,* a place where we could document the daily, weekly, and monthly operations and protocol developed for everything from phone calls, inquiries, and paperwork to therapy processes and operational details.

In both instances, I was searching for a way to convey vast amounts of information about how *Horse Sense* did business, while documenting important aspects and reducing repetition. An SOP manual would help train new people and clarify procedures. I began to wonder if it might also help answer questions for the people who called as well.

It wasn't until the 2006 Annual EAGALA Conference that it all came together. EAGALA trainer Mark Lytle of the Head, Heart, Hands, & Horses program in Marion, NC, knew people were coming to me for answers. He suggested that I put their questions together in a presentation for the Annual Conference event. It would be an opportunity to gather answers to some of the most common questions and talk about the things *Horse Sense* learned in the process of becoming a business.

As it turns out, the presentation was a catalyst and key opportunity. It helped to clarify that people didn't just need answers to their day-to-day questions; they were searching for answers to Big Picture issues that were even more crucial. I realized that the SOP manual was only the beginning. The presentation led to development of a seminar series, "Making EAP Work," and the writing of this book.

## **What** this book is

**H**orseman Pat Parelli has a famous saying: "Green on green makes black on blue." He is referring to the all-too-typical scenario of the green horseperson who buys a green horse, and the recipe for trouble that is sure to follow. When the person doesn't know anything and the horse doesn't know anything, well, you can guess the rest.

The same is true for the equine assisted business model. EAP/EAL businesses have a lot of moving parts. And, like buying your first horse, you can get into a lot of trouble very quickly when any one aspect of the business is lacking.

*Horse Sense, Business Sense* will talk about the early phase of establishing an EAP business, outlining basic choices, issues, and pitfalls in getting a business off the ground. The books that follow will then discuss the different challenges that face a business in the adolescent and mature stages. This book is primarily about the process of finding our way as an organization, and lessons we've learned in the process of practicing EAP and EAL. It's about the choices we made, why we made them, and how the implications of those choices led to various outcomes. It will be about decisions, both good and bad, that can maybe help show the way for somebody else.

And while this is only one road map out of the many possible routes you may choose, I hope to illustrate some of the sound, basic principles that need to be established when starting a business. In the end, setting up your own equine assisted practice is about decisions that only you can make. I hope to show you the choices available to you, and use our experience with *Horse Sense* as a real-life example. Knowledge is power. The more you learn, the better off you and your business can be. I hope this book can give you some guidance into that process.

You'll find something else in each chapter, items from what I call my "Un-Despair" file. When we first started out, some days were so overwhelming that it was hard to remember why I was doing all this. Things like finances and management and networking seemed to be outside of my comfort zone, and all of it proved extremely discouraging.

I realized then that I needed an immediate, tangible reminder of the power of what we do, and I needed to reach for that reminder without having to search. So I started the "Un-Despair" file, where I could keep inspiring letters, notes, and emails from clients and others speaking about what their experience at *Horse Sense* had meant to them. The Un-Despair file pulled me out of many hard days and still serves to give me a lift when I need

it most. While I've removed identifying information for client confidentiality, I thought you might also enjoy and be inspired by these. I encourage you to start your own Un-Despair file from the very start!

I hope there are others out there who, unlike me, already have a grasp of running a business. I started from the ground up. My background as an English teacher prepared me to do many things, but running a multi-employee business was not one of them. *Horse Sense* had several challenging handicaps right from the start, and I was at the top of the list!

So a few words about what this book is not. This is not a book that teaches business, finance, accounting, or banking. It is not about running an office,

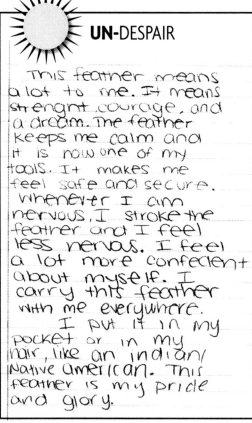

**UN-DESPAIR**

> This feather means a lot to me. It means strenght, courage, and a dream. The feather keeps me calm and it is now one of my tools. It makes me feel safe and secure. Whenever I am nervous, I stroke the feather and I feel less nervous. I feel a lot more confedent about myself. I carry this feather with me everywhere. I put it in my pocket or in my hair, like an indian/Native American. This feather is my pride and glory.

*A letter from a girl in a local boarding school, who found a turkey feather while out in pasture with the horses and took it home.*

how to be a good manager, or implementing organized systems. Neither is it a book of instruction about therapy, or how to do EAP or EAL. Most of all, it is not a course in horsemanship or horse care.

There are tremendous resources available for each of these disciplines, and I hope you take full advantage of them before you attempt to start your own EAP/EAL business. Institutions like S.C.O.R.E., the SBA, and local Chambers of Commerce are vital to a fledging business.

Organizations—like EAGALA (Equine Assisted Growth and Learning Association), NARHA (North American Riding for the Handicapped Association), EFMHA, Epona, EAPD, AIA, and EGEA—are at the forefront of the industry. Excellent systems for horsemanship exist from big names like Parelli to local teachers and experts. And don't forget your county extension offices, universities, and technical colleges for agriculture expertise, courses, and information.

In each chapter you'll find a few recurring items. One of them is a Recommended Reading list specific to the content of that chapter, be it business basics or horse care and farm management. These represent a "short list" of books that are key to the topic, although I may not have cited each one in the chapter itself. There is also a longer, more exhaustive Recommended Reading list in the back of this book. You can find links to purchase many of these books from the *Horse Sense* website.

Two additional things I recommend: a healthy dose of humility and a strong set of guiding principles. It doesn't take long to realize that no matter how experienced you are, it takes a lifetime of learning to run a business correctly. And it doesn't take long to get lost in the maze of choices and situations without guiding principles to lean upon. It's important that you have guiding principles, whether mine or your own. We'll talk more specifically about principles later on.

## The **New Face** of Therapy

**W**hile some may compare it to other forms of therapeutic practice, equine **assisted practices** involve additional aspects that make them both more alluring and more troublesome than any ordinary business. The first aspect to examine is the type of people drawn to the world of equine assisted practice.

A significant trend has been building in America's workforce since the 1990's, a trend that has perhaps accelerated since the cataclysmic events of 9/11. More and more people are looking for a way out of traditional 9-5 careers, and searching for work that instead feeds their greatest passions and inspirations. I suppose there is nothing new about this desire, but until now only a lucky few have had the privilege of indulging in work they love.

But that is changing. According to Candace Corner, a writer for CareerBuilder.com, Animal Assisted Therapy is one of the top ten cutting edge professional fields in 2007, alongside Veterinary Physical Therapists & Art Therapists. She notes that Animal Assisted Therapists "study and identify behavioral patterns in animals and apply techniques to improve mental, social and physical issues within humans through animal/human companionship." She states that a Bachelor's of Science degree in Psychology, Social Work, Physical Therapy, Nursing or Education are needed in addition to further training. She also refers to specialties within the field, such as Social Work, Education and elderly care.

Equine assisted practice holds that appeal for a unique cross section of people. The two main types of people who become interested in equine assisted therapy are therapists and horse people. And each has their unique set of challenges to overcome. In the case of *Horse Sense*, I fall into the category of being a non-therapist horse person running a therapy business.

For those who love horses, finding ways to make a healthy living with horses has always been a challenge. Traditional equine-based jobs are scarce, prone to great physical and financial risk, or reserved for the few who possess the talent to ride, train, or teach. For experienced people who fall into this category, equine assisted practice is an exciting and viable new way to make a career in a horse business. Horse people may face many challenges fitting into the structure a therapy business requires. And, while no stranger to physical risk, the horse person may fail to understand the implications of poorly executed therapy on a vulnerable client.

The other audience for equine assisted practice—and this book—is the mental health therapist looking for a better way. For those who are victims of burnout, bureaucratic red tape, or disaffected by traditional talk therapy, equine assisted therapy represents a stimulating field full of possibilities. Equine therapy is also a way to supplement their clients or help those for whom all other methods have failed. The challenge for non-horse people will be in learning how to get out of the office to be effective, and developing the necessary skills to work with horses . . . animals that require a different set of skills and understanding.

If there is one real source of danger to equine assisted practice as a viable form of work, it is perhaps the inexperienced therapist and the inexperienced horse person trying to work together. Already I've seen a dangerous trend in the number of people without appropriate therapy or horse experience saying, "Hey! I've got a curry comb and a horse, let's do some therapy!"

No matter which category you fall into, anyone entering this field is responsible for getting as much education as possible. Equine-based therapy work isn't as easy as it looks, and the pitfalls can be both deceptive and potentially devastating. The combined responsibilities of owning horses and facilitating the well-being of clients are serious.

## MY **STORY**

*M**y journey to equine assisted practice and horses in general is both personal and professional.***

*I grew up with my parents and a brother in Central Florida. My father was an influential community leader and philanthropist who created a highly successful manufacturing business. He passed away when I was sixteen, but his influence has helped to shape the work I do today.*

*My path to horses began as a child with a pony named Snowball, followed by years riding at summer camp, horse shows, and a brief stint with a horse of my own named Misty. But eventually I got more involved with band, school, and youth activities.*

*After high school, I earned a Bachelor's degree in Writing, Literature, and Publishing from Emerson and a Masters in English at the University of Florida. I met my husband Richard in 1993, and we moved to Dallas, Texas in 1994 after finishing my Masters. I began teaching in the community college system and entered academia full time. We married in 1996.*

*While my career centered on cerebral pursuits, it was not too many years before my interest in horses surfaced again. For me, getting back into horses represented a* need for a connection that never really went away, and eventually I started taking night classes in horseback riding at a local tech school, and lessons at a local barn. I also started doing volunteer work for a therapeutic riding facility in Texas, and became very excited . . . not so much about the physical element, which was amazing, but the emotional response and healing that I saw. However, I also saw firsthand the weaknesses and struggles involved in the operation of a volunteer non-profit organization.

Meanwhile, I realized immediately that things weren't as easy for me around horses as they had been when I was younger; I had far less trust and a lot more fear. Some of the horses I worked with were frustrating, challenging my self-image as a talented, level-headed, competent, college English professor. These challenges with my horses would eventually inform my understanding of horses as kind but firm teachers, if we will but listen.

The path to actually rehabilitating horses began with our move to North Carolina in 2000. Our stable of two horses, Masada and Susan Denero ("Black Eyed Sue"), began to grow as we rescued and rehabilitated horses assisting the Hope for Horses program in Leicester, NC. We adopted Gus, our retired police horse, and began adding more and more horses to our herd.

The Parelli horsemanship system came into the picture after I attended a Parelli tour stop in Atlanta in 2001. What impressed me was not how good the Parellis were with horses but how good their students were with horses. What I saw was that the Parelli method could be taught and transferred to others. They had a system that worked. I threw myself into the Parelli method after that.

I first began using the Parelli method as a diagnostic tool when working with horse rescue. We'd often get calls to pick up horses . . . but questions about how to catch horses without coercion, how to load physically emaciated horses in trailers, or how to safely travel with sometimes delicate minds and bodies were unanswerable. While there may be many ways to force these tasks, many involve taking away the horse's dignity, which is never an acceptable option. So much time is spent dealing with the physical horse that his emotional and mental state is not taken into account or is flat-out ignored. What I wanted, and what I got in the Parelli program, was a way of assessing the emotional fitness of the horse, to keep us all safe.

*Parelli's "Seven Games" became an excellent tool. Using them, I could gauge a horse's propensities, judge his reactions, and have a better gauge for knowing how and when a horse was safe to transport. That's how the Parelli philosophy became part of* Horse Sense.

## The Path to *Horse Sense*

**E**ventually the question of finding homes for unrideable horses came up. It was easy to find homes for young, rideable horses, and it was relatively easy to find retirement homes for old horses. But it was nearly impossible to find homes for young, *un*rideable horses. The rescue was becoming full of these animals, and making space for urgent cases was becoming an issue. How could we solve this problem of finding meaningful work and homes for horses like Gus, a horse who could no longer be ridden?

At the same time, as I was visiting with friends and acquaintances, I would talk about my horses, and the lessons they were teaching me. My friends started coming out, not to ride, but to get what I was getting from being around horses. Slowly I started to put the two together: horses that couldn't be ridden and people who didn't necessarily want to ride. I realized people could benefit from being around the horses without ever putting a foot in the stirrup. An Internet search led me to EAGALA, and I began reading about equine-based therapy online. Two months later I was attending my first training program in Hendersonville, NC.

I have to confess that my first impressions of equine therapy were not entirely favorable. While I was excited about the philosophy and approach of EAGALA, I saw many people there who were not exhibiting healthy patterns, and seemed to be, from the start, in this field for the wrong reasons. I was intrigued but still had a healthy dose of skepticism.

2002's EAGALA conference in San Diego began changing that. This particular conference was practical and tangible. For the first time, I saw real people working with real programs. I was inspired by other people's programs and their work for the benefit of both people and horses. I came away thinking "If this is what equine therapy is all about, this I can do." I came back from the conference, and began laying plans. *Horse Sense* opened in June 2003.

## **Building** *Horse Sense:*  MY **STORY** continued

**N**ow that I had made the decision, I had to formulate the business structure I wanted to follow. *Were we a training barn? A riding center? An EAP center? All three? Our first tagline, "For Those Seeking Harmony and Healing with Horses," shows how broad we were in the beginning . . . vague because we simply didn't know who we were. "Harmony" came from the Parelli system, and "Healing" came from my experience. I was happy with that tagline as a starting place, but eventually it proved too general.*

*While I toyed around with idea of going back to school for a Social Work degree, my real passion lay in being an Equine Specialist, which meant finding the other members of the team elsewhere. I knew I needed a therapist. In 2001 I met Lynn Clifford, a riding instructor studying to be a Licensed Professional Counselor and a staff member at the farm that hosted my first EAGALA training. She was in her intern-ship collecting hours toward her LPC. We crossed paths again in 2003, the same time I was looking for a therapist to start* Horse Sense.

*We decided to do a few tentative test pilot cases together. We started with one or two kids from the Madison County Friends of 4-H Youth organization, and after experiencing positive results, put on several demos in June and July. By September,* Horse Sense *hired another Equine Specialist and an accountant. It was September when we really began seeing clients.*

I'll repeat what I wrote earlier: depending on who you talk to, you'll either get the hopeful news or brutal truth about small businesses. It's tough to be a small business and stay afloat. The one thing we had at the beginning was that the farm already existed before we opened *Horse Sense*, including the arena, the horses, and the barn. The program, in fact, grew out of a desire to pair our rehabilitated and rescue horses to a purpose with people in need of therapy and rehabilitation. It was the horses that drove the initial idea.

Truthfully, if I had known the grim statistics, I might never been brave enough to do what I did. At the same time, had I known the statistics, I might have taken some aspects more seriously! For example:

**33% of all small businesses fail or close within the first two years**

**50% of all small businesses fail/close within the first four years**

These numbers contrast sharply with statistics in the table below, which reflects the amazing growth of the EAP and EAL field in recent years.

| | Outpatient Programs/ Day Programs | Inpatient/ Residential Programs | Total | Percentage Growth from Previous Year |
|---|---|---|---|---|
| 2000 | 34 | 9 | 43 | |
| 2001 | 106 | 19 | 125 | 191% |
| 2002 | 178 | 30 | 208 | 66% |
| 2003 | 246 | 32 | 278 | 34% |
| 2004 | 344 | 44 | 388 | 40% |
| 2005 | 389 | 48 | 437 | 13% |

Internationally, the number of Canadian programs doubled from 2000-2002, with 15 total programs as of 2005. Multiple programs exist in England, Scotland, Mexico, and Australia as of 2006, and Equine Therapy & Learning is being offered in South Africa, Peru, and Sweden. While the above numbers were taken solely from the EAGALA Annual Resource Handbooks 2000-2005, these figures reflect the enormous growth (almost 200% in one year!) and development of the field nationwide . . . and quite a lot of growth it is. And yet, although the growth is substantial, these figures don't account for the many businesses that fold each year.

## Making **Choices**, Seeking **Answers**

**W**hen you consider starting an equine-assisted program of your own, there are a multitude of choices and decisions that you need to make in every component of your therapy program. This chapter is devoted to giving you a bird's-eye view of those choices and options in every aspect of your EAP business. We'll then go into greater detail on each of these aspects further in the book. Here are the areas of your business you'll need to set up and organize:

✳ The business structure

✳ Your core program

* Equine management
* Team structure and philosophy
* Basic facility
* Guiding Principles and Systems

Here are some of the questions our examination will begin to address:
* Do you want to be a non-profit or a for-profit business?

* Should the business be a corporation, partnership or a proprietorship?

* What type of equine work do you want to do?

* What type of therapy do you want to do?

* What kind of clientele is required?

* What is the method of finding and handling horses?

* What type of staffing will be necessary?

And this is just some of the practical stuff. As you can see, there are many questions, and many choices to make. My recommendations are: do everything you can to study and learn. Find and utilize the resources available. Attend small business conferences. Attend therapy conferences. Visit other programs. Call people.

Pursue answers, and make your key decisions before you dig the first posthole, pour the first foundation, or spend that first dime. In other words, *know who you are*. As Pat Parelli says, "Take the time it takes, so it takes less time." It could also take less money and measurably less grief as well.

## So You Want to be an **Entrepreneur**?

**B**efore we begin, it might be helpful to ask yourself one simple question: do you really want to be an entrepreneur? Because whether you end up with a for-profit business or a non-profit program, that's what you'll be: an entrepreneur.

Just as this book was going to press, I came across an article in the business section of my local paper about recent trends for 2007: "It will be more and more difficult to be a successful entrepreneur. 'The zeal is there, but the cost of entry is so high,' Gerald Celente of The Trends Research Institute says. 'You need ... thousands of dollars to pay the government, insurance, and compensation. And, if you don't have a real niche, it's very tough to compete against the big boys.'" (*Asheville Citizen-Times*, 1/4/07)

So clearly the news is both good and bad. We are all part of a fast growing niche in the field of therapy and learning, but it's still a hard job to be an entrepreneur. In fact, it's getting more difficult all the time. I say this not to dissuade you, but to make sure you know what's in front of you, more so than I did. There are both high points and low points to being an entrepreneur, but knowing how hot or how cold the water is before jumping in is key! It also highlights the very serious need to do everything you can to set your business up correctly, right from the start.

**TOP REASONS TO START** YOUR OWN EQUINE ASSISTED BUSINESS:

1. EAP and EAL *work*, producing tangible results for clients.
2. Being able to do something you love.
3. Being able to witness amazing growth and change in people.
4. Being with the horses.
5. The view from the office window, which is pretty good!

**TOP REASONS *NOT* TO START** YOUR OWN EQUINE ASSISTED BUSINESS:

1. It is really hard to make a living, and make the business work.
2. Long hours.
3. The necessary evils of business, including all the time you'll spend in an office or out in the community, as opposed to outside with the horses.

## The Right Perspective, Right From the Start

**O**ne key concept you need to grasp before starting your business comes from one of my favorite books, Stephen Covey's *The 7 Habits of Highly Effective People*: "Begin with the end in mind."

Building a business is a lot like building a skyscraper. If you don't have the right foundational elements on the bottom, you compromise each and every layer on top, until the whole thing eventually collapses. With a skyscraper, the foundation is all about brick, mortar, and steel. The cornerstone of your business, on the other hand, is about the Business Plan, Vision, and Mission Statement.

Many people are intimidated at the thought of having to write their first business plan or write their vision and mission statements. Yet these three elements are crucial to building your foundation and setting the direction for everything that follows. They become the unifying concept that everyone understands and agrees to, and the shining star that guides you in becoming really clear about who you are. Having these three elemental pieces of your foundation in place before you get underway helps you to "begin with the end in mind" and puts you on the right track.

Did I "begin with the end in mind" when I started *Horse Sense*? As you will see later, and throughout this book, I discovered these valuable tools through trial, error, and hindsight. I urge you to begin that process now, no matter where your business is at, so you can course correct before going further.

I also want to talk here about another key business concept important for those laying the groundwork for a new business in any field: the concept of working on your business rather than in your business.

A year into operating *Horse Sense*, I was introduced to a book called *The E-Myth*, by Michael Gerber. I now think of it as required reading for everyone going into business for themselves. I didn't necessarily like everything I read, but right away it forced me to begin to look at the business in a very different way. I began thinking of *Horse Sense* from a long-term perspective. I suspect the material in this book may cause you to experience the same sense of discomfort; I urge you to listen to that discomfort . . . and remember the EAGALA concept "when you're outside your comfort zone, important learning can occur." You may find, upon examination, that there is much to consider here.

The overarching distinction Gerber makes is pointing out the difference between a "technician business" and an "entrepreneur business." In a technician business, someone who is highly skilled at a particular form of work starts their own business performing that skill for hire. It could be any number of skills, including carpentry, plumbing, photography, or equine assisted therapy. The mindset sounds something like this, "I'm really good at doing X. So I'm going to strike out on my own, and spend the rest of my time doing X." In order to survive, the person in the "technician business" is always dependant on their ability to perform. If they become incapacitated for any reason, workflow stops and the whole thing shuts down.

In an "entrepreneur business," on the other hand, other people perform the technician's duties while the business owner manages the business itself. Workflow is not dependent upon the business owner's capacity to do the work or provide the service, so they are free to keep the perspective necessary to manage the business' growth and long-term development. His or her energy is not solely spent keeping widgets in production, but in managing the flow, organization, and sales of that production. This is not to say the business owner can't also be a technician, but a clear distinction is important.

Working *in* your business means working as a "technician," executing the functions of getting the work done. Working *on* your business, however, is a very different thing. The business owner who doesn't understand this perspective is setting themselves up for a major case of burnout. The technician business is never able to grow beyond a certain point because the business is dependent on their limited ability as the technician to produce. Working as an employee and as a business leader are two different jobs, and without balancing the two, it won't be long before the business is running *you* . . . and running you into the ground.

In the early days of *Horse Sense*, I wasn't aware of this concept. I just simply opened the doors and started. I worked as the ES, the horse care person, and as the marketing, P.R., and finance people all rolled into one. And without knowing it, I was heading down a road for trouble. I now pay close attention to the time I spend being a technician—because that's the work that inspires and motivates me—and the time I spend running my business. I spend about 50% of my time focused on developing *Horse Sense* as a business: following up leads, writing grants, marketing, attending meetings, being visible in the community, doing demos and presentations. I have more "technicians" back at the farm, experts at seeing the clients and doing the job.

Certainly, you're going to be doing a lot of different jobs if you start your own business. Few of us can afford the luxury of hiring staff. Yet it is critical that you see, and establish, the difference between these roles. One executes work, the other looks into the future, lays the plans, and actively keeps the company on track from a sense of perspective. I recommend careful study of the concepts inside *The E-Myth*, and that you begin putting them into place before you go any further. It could be vital for your business' long-term health.

## Building a **Virtual Team**

**A**long those same lines, I highly recommend assembling a "Virtual Team" of people to execute the critical specialties necessary for your business' survival. The beauty of a Virtual Team is that they are contractors, not employees, and utilized on an as-needed basis. They are also specialists, trained professionals in the business community, who know how to execute their functions with optimum efficiency and— more importantly—results.

The first member of the *Horse Sense* Virtual Team was an accountant who specialized in work with artists, nonprofits, and out-of-the-ordinary businesses like ours. I knew finances were too important to screw up. Even though we're not a non-profit, her understanding of that world made her a good fit for our unique business.

The second member of the Virtual Team consisted of a graphic designer who helped us with our business logos, and was responsible for making sure ads were laid out, proofed and placed. The beauty of having her—and any Virtual Team member—is that the work just "happens." I can set the course, then trust that something professional, timely, and on-target will appear. My Virtual Team has slowly grown to include people to help me with my strategic plan, my marketing plan, finances and other areas.

Here again, most organizations try to "make-do," putting people already in the office to work at things like marketing or bookkeeping because they have a little bit of extra time, or because they once took a class in Photoshop and think they can lay out your brochure. The results always speak for themselves. While you may *think* that brochure doesn't look too bad, in reality the message inside is probably out of focus or off-target, and the graphics portray you like amateurs. Not exactly the image you want to create in the outside world . . . and in the end, money that's NOT doing the work it should. Ultimately, good money wasted.

Rather than trying to make square pegs fit in round holes, get people who are good at what they do! Finding and growing a Virtual Team of people from your community who are already experts in accounting, graphic design, writing, business planning, marketing, and public relations DOES cost money. But these same people know how to hit their mark with swiftness and efficiency that comes from years of expertise. They can set you on the right track, right away, and elevate you to a level of competence and professionalism that will put you light years ahead of your own make-do efforts.

Be prepared to shop around for your Virtual Team. Don't go with a web designer because she's the niece of your next-door neighbor. For each specialty, bid the work out—you'll be amazed at the variation in price, skill sets, and personalities—then interview several candidates. And whatever you do, don't go for the cheapest. Negotiate a fair price for the best *fit*, and you'll have a true resource.

Of course, you still need to manage your Virtual Team, using a global vision that directs their efforts. Finding that group of people who really *get* what you do and work well with your team is priceless. Once you've done the footwork of establishing good working relationships, your Virtual Team will always be there when you need them. And their efforts will free you to do what's most important: run your business. Now *Horse Sense* has a website designer who is amazing, another person who is doing Internet PR, and others who are doing different things that are making a big difference for the business.

## Funding and **Capital**

**B**rutal Truth Number One about starting a business: most small businesses **fail because of lack of capital.** If you're doing EAL work and getting paid at the time of services, it's good news to your bookkeeper. But if you're doing EAP work funded by health insurance or grants, be prepared for another paradigm . . . the paradigm of delayed payment and sporadic cash flow.

There are plenty of books and resources on how to find capital to fund your business. And certainly many equine therapy businesses start out winging it, providing services for free while raising money for the bare minimum for things like flyers and equipment. Problem is, even flyers require printing and mailing costs. A simple demo creates expenditure for food and drink. It always costs more than you expect.

The first priority for any organization is finding the money to go into business in the first place: start-up funding. Making progress in this phase oftentimes requires creating a pitch that that gets banks and sources of funding excited about your program. It's often easier to obtain start-up funding for an innovative idea than it is to obtain ongoing funding, because it's easier to get funding organizations excited about those innovative new ideas. It's also harder to writer a grant to get a tractor or a specific piece of equipment for your physical plant. Funding organizations tend to want their money to go to your after-school kids program, for example, and are less interested in funding the tractor or the farm or the building that makes the after-school program possible.

You might choose to raise funds yourself through "bootstrapping," the term for pulling yourself up by your boot straps with your own funding by calling upon friends, family, or your own resources to help get your business vision off the ground. This is what I did with the help of my dad's manufacturing business success. There is the category of funding called "Angels," which refers to people or organizations that specifically look to fund entrepreneurial/visionary companies. These people often-times are entrepreneurs themselves who want to reach out and help the new business coming up behind them. They are also usually people who can recognize a neat idea that may be "out of the box" when they see it. Then there is the broad category of outside sources: the Small Business Administration, your local bankers, community business incubators, and the like. Some addresses for these sources of funding are listed below, others are listed at the back of this chapter and book.

---

Here's a brief overview of start-up business resources:

**www.score.org**—SCORE "Counselors to America's Small Business" is a program that provides free business counseling to entrepreneurs. There are Chapter offices nationwide.

**www.onlinewbc.gov**—The Online Women's Business Center helps women start and build a successful business through counseling and teaching.

**www.sba.org**—The Small Business Administration (SBA) provides small business counseling and training through a variety of programs and resource partners. There are offices in many cities and states throughout the country.

**www.smallbusinessschool.com**—A soup-to-nuts organization that helps in every phase of small business start up and development, with extensive links to small business resources.

---

While there are several sources for small business loans in the for-profit realm, grants may be a crucial source of start-up funding if you go the non-profit route: funding may come through your local United Way or various community foundations. Just as with any commercial small business loan, having a good business plan is crucial for obtaining start-up funds via grants. You'll need financial projections and a road map to show your viability for the grant.

Your proposal at this stage needs to be about the Big Picture. In this scenario, you're trying to educate your funding source about the industry. You need to provide statistics to prove its worth in the world. Be constantly aware that explaining equine assisted practice is a real challenge, especially if you're dealing with people unused to thinking in these terms. So be prepared to support your explanation with visuals and language that explains how EAP and EAL work, and how it gets results.

Know too, that by accepting funding from community organizations, you may become accountable to that organization in a variety of ways. You may be required to perform due diligence by opening your books to regular audits, comply with certain parameters, prove the results of your program through various tracking means, or even lose personal control over parts of your program. Be sure you understand what barriers or requirements your funding may engender.

I'd like to invite you to start out taking your equine assisted practice as a serious business, and thinking differently, or at least differently than I did. Recognize, right away, that capital is important, and make sure you have as much as you can muster. Plan for it properly, and do the necessary groundwork so that you don't get caught in that number one Brutal Truth.

## **What** Kind of **Structure** Do You Want to Have?

*For-Profit vs. Non-Profit*

**I am often asked about the differences between establishing a program as a non-profit vs. for-profit business.** I went back and forth for long time on this issue, especially since I intended *Horse Sense* to simply break even or do modestly well financially. The main reason I chose a for-profit business over non-profit was influenced, again, by the fact *Horse Sense* existed in my backyard. I had both seen and heard of instances where a founder lost control of their property, or lost many friends when their non-profit's board of directors took over a program and began making decisions based on the best interest of the non-profit, and not the best interest

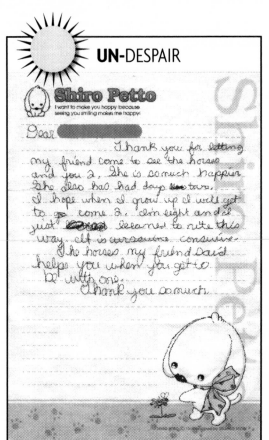

## UN-DESPAIR

### Shiro Petto
I want to make you happy because
seeing you smiling makes me happy!

Dear ▓▓▓▓▓▓▓▓

Thank you for letting my friend come to see the horses and you 2. She is so much happier. She also has had days too. I hope when I grow up I will get to come 2. I'm eight and I just become learned to rite this way. It is awesome. consuive. The horses my friend David helps you when you got to be with one. Thank you so much.

A letter we received in the mail from a friend of one of our clients.

of the founder's horses and farm. The chances of that happening are slim, but I didn't want to take that chance.

I've been a part of a lot of non-profit organizations, and I wanted to implement aspects of control that you can't always get with a non-profit organization. I wanted to employ strict standards of professionalism and accountability. In a volunteer-based organization, a culture of entitlement sometimes arises from volunteers who, along with a corresponding lack of account-ability, can create an attitude resembling something like this: "You should be grateful I'm here at all, much less doing it the way you want me to, in a timely fashion."

In my experience, it can be much more difficult to maintain a consistent, healthy, stable environment with a rotating roster of volunteers and a board of directors that come and go over the years. Each new board may implement changes of direction that disrupt the structure of the business. Board members and volunteers can burn out of trying to balance the organization's responsibilities with their real life, and keeping a steady supply of both becomes a full-time job on its own. I wanted a staff who could devote their professional skills to *Horse Sense* as their primary focus and responsibility. There are many fine non-profit EAP/EAL businesses out there, but I doubted *my* ability to run one. So I went the for-profit route.

I can't say I still don't go back and forth. One of the biggest detriments being a for-profit is the challenge of grant writing. Many grants you might be inclined to pursue only give to non-profits. So grants are a huge motivating factor in being a non-profit. There's a lot of opportunity in that area.

Being a for-profit organization does not keep *Horse Sense* from developing good relationships with our fellow non-profit equine organizations, however. I recommend establishing relationships with the other programs in your area, both non-profit and for-profit. Don't wait until the last minute to start talking to these groups. *Horse Sense* has successful partnerships with local non-profits to pursue grant money for funding JCPC programs. A local non-profit therapeutic riding program sponsors the grant, and then pays *Horse Sense* to provide EAP services to JCPC youth. As a for-profit business, *Horse Sense* works with the non-profit facility to create a situation that enables both programs to fund enhanced services to the population. It creates a win-win situation.

Partnering with other area equine therapy organizations does two things. It gives each organization the opportunity to be experts in their own field and prevents overlap of services. And it creates wonderful possibilities that help both organizations succeed in their mission.

## *Partnership, LLC, S-Corp, and C-Corp*

If you've decided to go the for-profit route, then you need to choose the structure of that business from the following options: Sole Proprietorship, Partnership, LLC's, S-Corps and C-Corp. A sole proprietorship and a partnership do not offer the protection from liability necessary in this field of work, because any debt or liability that belongs to the company also belongs to you personally, putting your personal assets at risk (not a great position to be in). A Partnership is exactly that, a business partnership between you and another person to run the business, often set up in various configurations and percentages of ownership. The degree of ownership is usually based on what you each bring to the business. Unless you have an enormously good reason (and an amazing relationship), I suggest you avoid the Partnership structure. There is just too much at stake, both for your business and your relationship. A C-Corp is a business entity typically used by big business, the kind that finances itself in part by being open to the public through stock buy-in. It is an unlikely place for most of the people reading this book to begin.

It is quite likely that you'll be forming either a Limited Liability Corporation (LLC) or an S-Corp, so we'll spend a bit more time comparing these two. They are similar in that they are both "pass-through" entities for tax purposes, meaning that the income from both types of company is passed through to you, the owner, to report on your personal income tax (you won't need a separate tax return for your business: Yeah!). But the differences between the two mainly involve complexity and flexibility. The LLC is more flexible and less complex, but there are more tax benefits to you with an S-Corp. This is where your attorney can best advise you, based on what your situation is and what you want to do. At our farm we have both structures: Meadows Town, LLC, comprised of my husband and myself, holds the property, the barns & arenas, and the horses; *Horse Sense* is an S-Corp that rents from the LLC.

When we set up *Horse Sense*, we gauged every decision by one primary factor: that we were operating the program out of our backyard. We didn't ever want our activities as *Horse Sense* to put our property at risk. Maintaining our home and animals was our priority. So the first thing we did was create layers of protection to insulate and isolate *Horse Sense*, as much as possible, from our home and farm. My husband and I have our house and a few acres surrounding it in our name; all the rest of the acreage is held by Meadows Town, LLC.

The differences between an S-Corporation and a Limited Liability Corporation are outlined extensively in many standard business books, but to truly understand the differences, advantages, and disadvantages of each, you should consult with a lawyer to set up the best configuration for your program. My consultants advised us to set up our program based on our situation and comfort level, and yours will too. So hopefully our horses will always be our horses, and our backyard will always be our backyard.

## Inpatient **vs.** Outpatient

**A**nother key decision to address early in the process is to determine what type of equine therapy organization you want to become. And here again, the options encompass a broad spectrum of possibilities that can confuse the public and cost you time and money if you don't clarify them early in the process.

Most equine assisted programs opt for an outpatient model in delivering services. Inpatient programs are more rare, entailing extensive legal, financial, and organizational structure requirements that typically outstrip the reason most people get into this business to begin with. If you intend to provide inpatient therapy services, I recommend you study and analyze existing programs with great care.

## The Equine **Therapy Continuum**

**J**ust like having a clear business plan, mission statement, and vision, making a clear decision about what type of equine assisted program you will practice is truly crucial to the success of your business long term. It gives you the touchstone and theoretical underpinning for everything else.

Two factors stand out right away as instrumental in your choice of program:

1. Determining which population you want to serve, and

2. Determining if your program will offer any riding of horses.

I believe it's important to know and understand the various theoretical models of equine assisted practices, and what their key differences are. Everybody has their own way of doing things and their own philosophical approach. It may be that you pick and choose to create your own unique program, or it may be that you find you're a perfect fit for one model over another based on the population you serve and the way you integrate your horses. I feel that making an informed decision is truly crucial to the success of your business in the long term. Having a theoretical home gives you a basis for everything else you do. It will also give you the company and support of other professionals practicing the way you are, which can be invaluable. The most important thing is to build a good understanding of the different approaches out there. Without exploring the whole field you can't know which model is right for you. Find out where you belong.

The big point of distinction within the field is Equine Assisted (or Facilitated) Psychotherapy (EAP) and Equine Assisted (or Facilitated, or Guided) Learning (EAL). EAP is specifically psychotherapy or mental health-related, performed with a mental health professional, and EAL is usually devoted to personal or professional growth, which can include corporate teambuilding, leadership development, life skill-building, and coaching. Beyond that, here's an overview of the three main programs in the United States today that offer training and certification of some sort within the field of Equine Therapies and Learning.

## EAGALA

Founded in 1999 by Lynn Thomas and Greg Kersten, the Equine Assisted Growth and Learning Association is a non-profit organization developed to "address the need for resources, education, and professionalism in the field of Equine Assisted Psychotherapy." The Vision of EAGALA states that the organization is "dedicated to improving the mental health of individuals, families, and groups," placing it firmly in mental health & psychotherapy. The tenets of EAGALA include brief, solution-focused therapy, and a team-centered approach with a three-fold philosophy that includes these tenants: 1) change occurs when people are outside their comfort zone, 2) people don't change unless they are challenged, and 3) that the most effective change occurs if they find their own answers to their questions. As of 2006, EAGALA therapy takes place 100% on the ground, and, as of 2007, the standards, ethics, and certification structure has been completely revamped to include more rigorous and definitive standards. EAGALA offers several levels of training, and supervision is instrumental to certification. (www.eagala.org)

## EFMHA/NARHA

Founded by Barbara Rector and Boo McDaniel, the Equine Facilitated Mental Health Association is a sub-section of NARHA (short for North American Riding for the Handicapped Association). EFMHA practices include both psychotherapy and learning. EFMHA has been in the process for several years of setting standards of certification for therapists and the horse professionals who wish to practice Equine Facilitated Psychotherapy (EFP). This recently resulted in a series of pilot Horse Professional trainings in 2005. In EFP as practiced by EFMHA, sessions may involve "handling, grooming, longeing, riding, driving, and vaulting," and sessions may or may not involve a team approach. They continue to set standards for all aspects of practicing EFP, and offer training and testing for those wishing to study this field (www.narha.org).

## Epona

Epona Equestrian Services was founded by Linda Kohanov in 1997. The "unique, multi-disciplinary approach" of Equine Facilitated Experiential Learning (EFEL) utilized at Epona Equestrian Services can include riding, energy work, and art therapy, among other offerings. Many of these workshops are facilitated by Epona Approved Instructors, those who've completed the apprenticeship program. Linda herself writes about working with a licensed mental health professional, Kathleen Barry Ingram, in both of her books, *The Tao of Equus* and *Riding Between the Worlds*. The Epona Approach™

does not train people to engage in psychotherapy, although those Epona Approved Instructors who are already licensed mental health professionals can choose to integrate their Epona training with their mental health work (www.taoofequus.com).

Beyond these three, there are many other disciplines and schools of thought, with more developing all the time:

✳ Among those that offer training opportunities, internships, and/or apprentice-ship programs include Equine Assisted Personal Development (EAPD), developed by Chris Irwin, which "involves the horse directly as a teacher." His books *Horses Don't Lie* and *Dancing with your Dark Horse* are excellent introductions to his particular philosophies and approach.

✳ The same is true for Barbara Rector's *Adventures in Awareness: Learning with the Help of Horses*, which can introduce you to the tenets and distinctions of her approach.

✳ Minnesota Linking Individuals, Nature, and Critters (MNLINC) is another source for learning programs that incorporate all of nature, including horses (www.mnlinc.org).

✳ Arianna Strozzi, author of *Horse Sense for the Leader Within*, is founder of the Equine Guided Education Association, an organization whose mission is "to create a unified discourse involving the interaction of the horse as a respected 'guide' in human growth, learning, and development" (www.egea.org).

✳ Another program is the OK Corral, founded by Greg Kersten. (www.okcorralseries.com).

✳ Colleges and Universities offering curriculums in the equine assisted field include Prescott College (www.prescott.edu), Naropa University (www.naropa.edu), and several universities throughout the country.

## Why EAGALA?

*H*orse Sense **has found the Equine Assisted Growth and Learning Associa-tion (EAGALA) model to be its home,** with a philosophy and doctrine that we feel most comfortable adopting. We follow the EAGALA model for a variety of reasons, but most importantly because they are committed to the team approach, dedicated to mental health, and because we subscribe to a similar philosophy of facilitating change.

The team approach is crucial, in our opinion, because it defies the traditional "power dynamic" of the one expert—the therapist—who has the answers, and instead utilizes multiple points of view. We believe that four eyes are better than two, and that in the team approach, we model effective and healthy communication for clients in our interactions. We are also primarily a mental health program, and believe we can best help our clients and serve our horses by having clients remain on the ground at all times. More will be said about our preference for 100% unmounted work later in this chapter.

Finally, the EAGALA philosophy of what causes change is most in line with our own. Change, in our experience, is usually sparked by discomfort or pain of some sort, such as being "sick and tired of being sick and tired." It's challenging and often uncomfortable to step outside our norms, but we believe that's where meaningful, lasting change begins. Using EAGALA's model also puts the human facilitators in the right perspective, i.e., *not* the most important element of the session. The *Horse Sense* team acts as "table setters," putting out the plates and the forks and the knives, but leaving the meal itself in the client's hands. We're there to help put everything together, but ultimately the "good stuff" is up to the horse(s) and the client.

*Horse Sense* spent a great deal of time exploring different programs in the beginning, attending EAGALA conferences, Epona seminars, and studying with Adele and Deborah McCormick, authors of *Horse Sense and the Human Heart*. We also attended an EFMHA pilot training and a NARHA annual conference. All of this was expensive, but crucial to our development. *Horse Sense* continues to study other methods and philosophies as they develop because equine assisted practice itself is still evolving as a field of study. Like anything else in life, it would be foolish to become rigid and inflexible when everything around us is still so fluid.

## To Ride or Not to Ride

*Horse Sense* is a non-mounted therapy program, which became a key aspect to choosing EAGALA as the program model. There are a variety of opinions on the mounted vs. unmounted issue. But there is no question that when introducing riding as a variable to the therapy equation, it changes the horse-human dynamic in many ways. For *Horse Sense*, it was a big topic of discussion. But, the difference in the horse-human relationship when mounted, and the fact that our horses can't physically be ridden, helped cement the decision.

When clients are mounted, it can shut down both the client's and the horse's ability to respond. Quite often, when a person saddles up, he or she starts focusing on not falling off, and ceases to listen to the feedback the horse is giving. Also, whether they believe it or not, the rider is often in a position of power and control over the horse, and can hurt the horse. We choose to remove this dynamic entirely. Finally, when the horse has a rider, his ability to escape without causing himself or his rider harm is limited; in effect we circumscribe the horse's ability to react. Since we are seeking precisely that—the horse's reaction—we don't want to set up a situation in which we would limit or muffle the horse's response. Nor do we want the focus to shift from the sometimes emotional and messy work at hand so that it becomes about riding. We wanted to remove that as an issue, by having no riding at all.

Having people ride requires teaching them, and we don't want to teach them when there are plenty of places and people out there doing a fine job already; we choose instead to specialize in work on the ground. We are able to point people interested in therapeutic riding to our sister organization, who specializes in it.

## Handling the Horses

Like choosing the appropriate philosophical model for your program, choosing a philosophical approach to handling your horses is important as well, and is often an overlooked structural element to therapy programs. Choosing a philosophy is important because there are so many philosophies—and strong opinions—that come into play from one horse person to the next.

Your organization would benefit from having a really clear approach to managing your equine herd, for your horses' sake if nothing else. Look around, and you'll start realizing how extensive individual philosophies and experience levels can be, from feeding to ground skills to training. Would *you* want to be a horse if each person you encountered handled you in a different way, or had completely different expectations? Your horses need the confidence that comes from consistent treatment, day in and day out, no matter who works with them. Any given program might have 2-10 different ES employees handling their horses; it's important to know they're all operating on the same page.

For *Horse Sense*, choosing our horse-handling model was easier than choosing our program model. Our purpose was both practical and philosophical. We wanted a common language for our horses, so that we could discuss, within certain parameters, every aspect of their management from a common viewpoint. If one horse develops an issue, we can automatically rule out certain things by knowing he has been handled in a certain way. This doesn't mean our system is foolproof; but it does simplify things a great deal.

When in question, our horse philosophy defines every aspect of our understanding as a team. In fact, it expands into one of our key client philosophies: the way we treat the client is the way we treat the horse, and vice versa. And if we ever catch ourselves doing something with a horse we would feel uncomfortable having our mothers see, perhaps we shouldn't be doing it. How we do anything is how we do everything. If we're doing something negative in our treatment of the horse, we might perhaps be treating clients inappropriately or without the dignity, respect, and integrity they deserve.

## Natural **Horsemanship**

**T**here are a variety of Natural Horsemanship practitioners and methods out there, and I strongly encourage anyone considering this field to become aware of the basic philosophies involved in the practice. Some of the forerunners in this field are Tom Dorrance, his brother Bill Dorrance, and Ray Hunt. Others include Monty Roberts, John Lyons, Buck Brannaman, Mark Rashid, and Pat & Linda Parelli. Although the specific approaches may vary, the principles and philosophies are key to the way *Horse Sense* practices Equine Assisted Psychotherapy and Learning. *The Revolution of Horsemanship* by Dr. Robert Miller is a valuable resource for those becoming familiar with the basics of Natural Horsemanship. I also recommend Dr. Miller's *Understanding the Ancient Secrets of the Horse's Mind* to inform from the horse's point of view.

I knew from the outset that Parelli Horsemanship was going to be our operating model for managing and handling our herd; I was committed to the Parelli approach before I became involved in EAGALA. The philosophy of "Love, Language, and Leadership" as opposed to Force, Fear, and Intimidation is an extraordinarily deep theoretical underpinning for the whole program.

When there is a question about the horses, we have a philosophy to refer to that sets us firmly in the "Natural Horsemanship" field, and defines every aspect of our understanding as a team. It reduces the amount of friction and politics surrounding horse handling and care, and quite frankly this simplifies things quite a bit. Our care and treatment of the horses is based upon a philosophy we all follow. Our base standard for Equine Specialists is Parelli Level I and EAGALA Level I.

Parelli is ideal for our rescue and rehabilitation horses because of its heavy focus on groundwork, psychology, and behavior. Beyond giving our team a common language, the Parelli and the EAGALA certifications are nothing more than a license to learn. A candidate's willingness to attain these certifications shows me the level of commitment a potential employee might have. It's the starting point for a long course of study.

## Handling the Team: Various Philosophies and Systems

**J**ust as our core program has a guiding philosophy, and our equine management has a guiding philosophy, it should be no surprise that our team at *Horse Sense* operates under a guiding philosophy which governs how we conduct business and interact with each other.

The EAGALA model of equine therapy automatically draws together people from very diverse backgrounds; the differences between the therapists and equine specialists alone can create quite a dichotomy. Within *Horse Sense* itself we have a wide range of varying backgrounds, age levels, and experience, all of which is fodder for some interesting team interaction. Without a guiding set of principles, this variety can spawn areas of potential conflict.

At *Horse Sense* in the early years, we decided the guidelines of Alcoholics Anonymous (AA) formed the best core philosophy for our team interactions. As with the Parelli system, I think it necessary to look outside ourselves and our personal biases to form choices and decisions grounded in a proven, concrete structure that puts all of us on the same playing field. This structure informs how we communicate with one another despite vast differences in belief systems, backgrounds, and personal styles.

AA is our preferred system at *Horse Sense*, but you could choose among several team-building models and philosophies. I know offices or organizations that function on other models, such as Miguel Ruiz's *The Four Agreements*, Stephen Covey's *The 7 Habits of Highly Effective People*, or Marcus Buckingham and Donald O. Clifton's *Now, Discover Your Strengths*.

## Handling the Facility

Equine therapy programs run the gamut when it comes to size, configuration, and operational models. It all depends on the circumstances. Programs can become massive in size and sophistication. Others are literally backyard operations with one or two people and a horse. You can rent, you can own, you can travel to separate facilities. Programs are hindered only by the creativity of the people operating them. And obviously, this same range of size and scope can pose challenges to a program's credibility, stability, and longevity. We'll be discussing more specifics of your facility in Chapter Four, but we'll touch on some key elements here.

Liability and confidentiality are the two top things that come to mind when talking about how to set up your program facility. Confidentiality, especially, becomes more of an issue in EAP work. There are several ways you can set up the facility, although the two most common are to use your own (or your ES's) backyard, or to rent another facility. Often the Equine Specialist's farm will become the facility, if for no other reason than that's where the horses are! It is fairly easy to set up and conduct sessions in this setting, especially if you are starting out part-time, seeing clients on evenings and weekends after day jobs. It is fairly easy to control confidentiality and weather-related concerns in these circumstances. If you are renting another facility part or full time, things become more challenging.

How do you conduct EAP and EAL out of a rental barn? Very carefully, and with lots of clear communication among all parties on the front end of the arrangement. When we first opened, we thought perhaps therapy would only be part of the business. Maybe we would board and hold any number of other smaller side businesses not specific to EAP. But we soon decided differently, namely because of the privacy and confidentiality issues of our clients. The more we looked at it, the more we realized that it would be less than ideal to try to operate other types of businesses out of the barn while maintaining client confidentiality. In doing EAP the barn becomes the equivalent of a doctor's office. Privacy, security, and emotional "safe space" issues all apply. You can't always accommodate these issues when the barn isn't your own.

If you go to a psychiatrist's waiting room, you *will* see other clients there—there's nothing they can do to protect your confidentiality in the outer confines of the waiting room, and the same is true for a barn. But once in session, providing appropriate emotional safety, total concentration, privacy, and lack of interruption are important for the client.

On one hand, the lack of privacy at a more public facility might be used to your advantage, creating a pretense that helps conceal the fact psychotherapy is taking place. On the other hand, you can erode credibility—and effectiveness—by conducting private work in an atmosphere that's not appropriate to the work. Overall, if you work out of someone else's barn, do so with a very clear understanding of what can and cannot take place at the barn—and where—when you are working there as the EAP team.

With EAL at a rental facility, the dynamics might change, but in different ways depending on the kind of work. For training or teambuilding sessions with business clients, your facility might need to reflect an image that satisfies a more corporate aesthetic. Buildings and fences need to be in top repair, equipment in mint condition, a staff that behaves as professionals, and a sense of strong organization in everything from the feed room to scheduling. This is not to say the opposite is true of EAP, but even in a barn setting, business professionals can recognize good management. Renting a facility might not give you enough control of those elements.

The rent-or-not-to-rent question also comes into play with liability concerns that exceed the scope of normal equestrian activities. *Horse Sense*, for example, works with a lot of juvenile justice kids who have serious and potentially dangerous issues. As a result, we must take into account that the safety of our property could be compromised by providing treatment in a place that is also our home. Am I worried about these clients coming here, seeing where I live and seeing where my horses live? How do I handle the concern for my horses and our own safety? We are cautious and aware of everything that happens on the farm. If you were providing treatment to the same type of clientele in your program, it would also be a huge factor in a rented facility.

## Overarching **Paradigms**

**I**cannot emphasize enough that your program needs to operate on clear principles and models. At *Horse Sense*, our therapeutic philosophy is EAGALA. Our horse philosophy is Parelli. And our inter-office philosophy is based on the principles of AA. When you have a lot of complex moving parts, each part needs to have its feet on firm ground. Feel free to adopt *Horse Sense's* guiding principles . . . but be sure to adopt *something* you can believe in. And stick with it.

Here's a few of the other *Horse Sense* **Guiding Principles** you'll be seeing throughout the book:

✱ **When in doubt ask the horse.** Whenever you're not sure what to do, ask the horse, and use his reaction as your guide.

✱ **How we would treat the horse is how we should treat client, and vice versa.** The horse and client are mirrors of each other.

✱ **If it's about us, we're doing it wrong.** In EAP work, our sessions always, *always* need to be about the horse and the client. As AA would say, "principles before personalities."

## Recommended **Reading** and Key **Websites**:

*4 Obsessions of an Extraordinary Executive*, Patrick Lencioni

*E-Myth Revisited*, Michael Gerber

*E-Myth Physician*, Michael Gerber

*Good to Great*, Jim Collins

*Non-Profit for Dummies*, Stan Hutton and Frances Phillips

*The One Page Business Plan*, Jim Horan

*Owner's Manual for Small Business*, Rhonda Abrams

*Revolution in Horsemanship*, Dr. Robert Miller

*Small Business for Dummies*, Eric Tyson and Jim Schell

www.AngelsCapitalAssociation.org

www.accessphilanthropy.com

www.grants.gov

www.smallbusinessschool.com

www.sba.gov/gopher/Local-Information/Certified-Preferred-Lenders

www.sba.gov/INV

www.sba.gov/sbdc

www.score.org

www.sba.org

www.smallbusinessschool.org

www.onlinewbc.gov

## Recommended Reading for EAP/EAL field in general:

*Horses Don't Lie*, Chris Irwin

*Horse Sense & the Human Heart*, Adele and Deborah McCormick

*Introduction to Equine-Assisted Psychotherapy*, by Patti J. Mandrell

*It's Not About the Horse*, Wyatt Webb

## Building a **Business System:**  MY **STORY** continued

**R**ichard and I never went into equine assisted practice with the idea of making money, but with the idea that we might make a living. We had both left fairly decent jobs: I was a college professor, and Richard was in computer programming and telecommunications. We never intended to make our horse business into a lucrative enterprise; we hoped to make a difference, and to make ends meet.

Amazingly, we also never intended to set up Horse Sense as a full scale business at the farm. We started out having an arena and horses, but as the program grew it became a necessity to set up a more serious structure around the business. Since we were operating in our backyard with our horses, we recognized the need to develop layers of protection between us and any possible event that might jeopardize it. More protection is better than less, and using the configuration we developed works out pretty well. By doing what we did, we always have a little control over our backyard.

On the advice of our lawyer, we set up a land-holding business called Meadows Town, LLC (Limited Liability Corporation), an entity that primarily exists as Richard's business. Meadows Town, LLC holds the bulk of our 90-acre property on which Horse Sense operates, with the exception of our house and a couple of surrounding acres, which are in our personal names. Meadows Town owns every part of the property where clients or horses are; Horse Sense then rents that from Meadows Town.

We set up Horse Sense itself as an S-Corporation, a business entity that operates by renting the facility, property, and the horses from Meadows Town, LLC. With this added layer of insulation in place, my comfort level is met so that I know my horses and my farm will not be jeopardy because of the work we're doing.

This structure also frees us up to develop other "profit centers" through Meadows Town, LLC, and outside the Horse Sense business. For example, in the process of working with large numbers of rescue dogs and horses, we became a big consumer of feed, vitamins, and minerals. We bought these items in such bulk that we ended up becoming a distributor. And, because we grow our own hay, the 14 acres of hayfields have become another source of income. So far none of these little enterprises really add up to anything significant, but all of it together lets us pay the bills.

# The **Business Plan**

**S**o here we return to the first piece of advice from Chapter Two, and one that I know many people are tempted to ignore: have a clear business plan. I should know; I was one of those who just simply started doing business without anything that resembled a plan. While business plans are not very sexy, they are absolutely necessary. And while it's not an overwhelming amount of work, the process has been mystified and complicated to the point where many people simply can't face the thought of writing one.

Well, it turns out there's a *lot* of stuff about running your own business that's not very sexy, a lot of things that aren't much fun. I never thought that marketing or networking were things that I would do. I never realized how many hours I'd spend behind my desk instead of working with my horses. I always felt that my good intentions would be sufficient to make it work, and I assumed that because I wasn't borrowing money from a bank, I didn't need a business plan. I was flat out wrong.

Even if you don't feel like you're a business person, even if you just want to help people, you probably won't be in existence long enough if you don't have a business plan. So let's take a quick look at what that entails.

Quite simply, a business plan forces you to get thoughts out of your head and onto paper. And at its heart, a business plan is nothing more than a process that obliges you to look at the basic tenants of running a business. Who are you serving? Where do your clients come from? How will you measure success? What are you trying to achieve? Where will the money come from? How will it be handled? Putting your thoughts on paper gives everyone on your team the chance to join you on the same page, to align themselves with goals, objectives, and strategies. And, once these things are out of your head, you can experience the freedom of having space for other things!

So after you draft a business plan, what do you do with it? Next to failing to create it, most people make the second most common mistake afterward: they throw it in a drawer and never look at it again. A business plan is a living document. It's meant to grow, change, and be adapted. The objectives are meant to be turned into action steps and budget items broken down by calendar months, by campaign, by team member, or however you want to distribute tasks and set up accountability. The point is to *use* it. Be guided by it. Know when you're on track, or when things begin to drift. Put out fires while they're still sparks instead of burning walls of flame. Measure your aspirations against reality.

There are some terrific resources for writing business plans. For those of you who experience true paralysis at the thought of writing a business plan, take a look at Jim Horan's book, *The One Page Business Plan* (onepagebusinessplan.com). It doesn't get any easier than this, a one-page document that at the very least forces you to think the process through in a simple step-by-step method. The book even comes with electronic documents and exercises on a CD-ROM. All you have to do is fill in the blanks.

I also recommend Barbara J. Scott's *Equine Assisted Psychotherapy Business Planning Guide & Workbook*. It's an excellent book, a valuable resource, and the only one I know of designed specifically for equine assisted businesses and organizations. Don't start your EAP/EAL business without consulting it.

You need a real business plan in place. Had I run the numbers before starting the business, it would have been enormously beneficial. I would love to have looked at what I projected I'd be making! I would have been forced to be more clear, so that my choices would also be clear. I could have been more centered, and hence better prepared for the surprises.

## **Zoning** Hot Buttons

**P**robably some of our biggest lessons in regard to *Horse Sense* as a business and equine facility had to do with zoning issues. Obviously, you need to make sure your business is properly zoned, especially if you plan to do it in your back yard. Don't move forward developing until you can be confident that you have ironed out all zoning issues. Run away from any contractor who tells you following local zoning ordinances isn't necessary. Perform due diligence on every aspect of your construction and operation zoning issues; do what's necessary in order to operate within regulations.

Be aware that sometimes zoning issues go beyond your local zoning board. When the neighbors around us learned of our plans, a whole drama unfolded over the fact we would be doing psychotherapy, working with troubled people, and especially high-risk youth. They were worried about grandmothers living alone, children at play. The drama created a series of hurdles that had to be cleared just with the neighborhood alone. However, the whole experience ended up working in our favor.

First, we had to submit a request to change the zoning in our area from Residential-Agriculture to Residential-Business, as I was instructed I needed to do. I sent a letter to the zoning board and introduced our services to them. We focused on promoting the unique and inventive way the property was being adapted, how we were proponents of keeping rural America looking rural and beautiful. We weren't trying to be a big business; rather we were operating a horse-based, agricultural business that would be a good neighbor to those around us.

We then scheduled a series of demonstrations geared towards neighbors, the sheriff department, the fire department, the Chamber of Commerce, and the zoning board . . . everyone we could think of. We had good turnouts of 20-30 people almost every time. The demos, combined with food, drink, and a dose of good neighborliness, helped ease tensions and went a long way toward clearing up the misunderstandings.

Had it been handled incorrectly, our zoning issues could have been a hot button that put *Horse Sense* in real jeopardy. It took a lot of hard work, but the episode forced us to get to know everybody, both on the zoning board and throughout the neighborhood. I ended up knowing people I never would have known, and eventually earning their goodwill and support. Ultimately, the Zoning Board agreed that Residential-Business didn't fit with what we were doing, so we proceeded as Residential-Agriculture. We even made the paper in the form of a political cartoon!

## Liability and Insurance Issues

### Program and Farm Liability

**First, whether you rent or use your own property, the farm itself should have it's own farm liability.** If this is your farm, the farm and program liability may be one in the same. If you rent, the stable you rent from should have this liability, and you should ask that your program be named as an additional insured on their policy. This is usually a simple matter for them and you. You should also then have them listed as an additional insured on your program liability, if that is possible with the way your program liability is set up. Some program liability is specific to the program itself, others are attached legally to all the individual practitioners of the program.

When it came time to develop the liability paperwork for *Horse Sense*, I consulted a lawyer, who was found through the North Carolina Horse Council, to develop a liability agreement for the business. I was lucky to find someone in North Carolina who dealt strictly with equine law, and with his advice drew up a waiver that every client signs. We have the basic NC Equine Statute posted in our barn as required. We also went through a process of developing, using, and then dropping a "Safety Contract" form of horse handling and barn rules for clients.

When it comes to insurance coverage for your facility, your business, and your professional staff, the world for equine assisted practice has been changing since it began. At *Horse Sense* we've always been extremely clear about the type of work we do. Our insurance in 2003 was extraordinarily simple and easy. Since then, I've heard industry rumblings from many programs about trouble over finding insurance coverage. We were grateful not to lose ours sooner, and know it will continue to be a challenge until credibility for the field has been firmly established. But the landscape is changing so rapidly that I never have any idea what will happen when our insurance comes up for renewal.

Any insurance agent can tell you what insurance companies are most concerned about: the Unknown Claim. It's that "unknown" aspect about EAP that causes insurance companies to balk. While other horse businesses have numerous liability issues with horseback riding, such as falls and accidents, the insurance industry is nonetheless more comfortable with their issues because they are *known*, defined, understood. What liability looks like for equine assisted psychotherapy is an unknown in comparison. And rightly so; I can understand their perspective.

Logic would say it's much more dangerous to throw an inexperienced person on horseback than to help that same person develop a relationship with the horse from the ground. Yet insurance companies hear that you're going to take an at-risk youth and put them with a thousand pound prey animal. Great! What they *don't* hear is that we're not riding. In fact, they don't know what we do. It's this "mysterious" aspect that we're in charge of explaining in un-mysterious ways.

Other forms of nontraditional practice have had to fight the battle of establishing themselves with the insurance industry, including chiropractic and acupuncture. Now it's our turn. One of the challenges for our industry is educating the insurance companies—both those that insure our programs and those that we might bill for services—about what we do and how we do it. We need to establish, communicate, and prove our standards. And we definitely need to minimize those programs that operate on a "fly-by-night-curry-comb-and-a-horse" mentality.

Insurance companies are responding to a lack of cohesive standards. Organizations like EAGALA and EFMHA are working to establish certification standards and best practices industry-wide, putting teeth into defining the difference between EAP, EAL, and other types of equine practices. Does equine therapy happen in the backyard with a horse and a curry comb? Absolutely. Is it billable to insurance companies? Maybe. Certain standards need to be in place for this to be a known, understandable commodity. I suspect that if we were to look at the history of "play therapy" one might see a very similar trajectory about how long it took to get recognized and understood in the industry.

Even though the process is going to take time regardless of how willing the insurance industry becomes, the duty for us, as practitioners, is to develop clear standards and language to talk about who we are and what we do. Educating insurance companies is part of what we need to do: invite them to participate in equine assisted practice, and find ways to talk to decision makers in the industry. The difference in standards and practices between EAGALA, Epona, and EFMHA need to become very clear. The more clarity about what the organizations are, the better off we all are.

### Professional Liability for Mental Health Professionals

Beyond the issues of insurance coverage for your business, you need to consider professional liability in the form of your licensed therapists. I wouldn't hire a therapist who didn't already have their own individual insurance, and if they're a licensed professional, insurance is easily obtained through professional organizations. Anyone in the process of getting their supervisory hours is not covered by insurance under their supervisor's insurance. They have to have their own insurance. Don't work without it.

Again, I feel it's very important to become aware of what's going on in the name of equine therapy within our individual communities. In Asheville, there is currently a therapeutic animal stewardship cooperative, a business that does work along the lines of Linda Kohanov's Epona work, an individual Epona-trained instructor offering personal growth and development, and several therapeutic riding programs. By being in contact with each other as professionals, we can work together to stay aware of the less credible organizations calling themselves equine assisted practitioners, the ones that should have most of us worried.

When something bad happens within less credible programs in our community and in our field, we all get hurt. As a former avid cave diver, I often compare EAP/EAL to cave diving. Cave diving is not a weekend sport, nor should it be. Nine out of ten reported "cave diving fatalities" aren't true cave divers, they're untrained open water divers who died because they ventured into a cave. Yet, inevitably the media reports "cave diver dies in cave accident," damaging the field of those who are credible and well-trained. It doesn't mean cave divers don't die in caves, but by in large it's not cave divers who are dying . . . its untrained, open water divers.

And like cave diving, equine therapy *looks* deceptively easy. An untrained diver will think, "The water is so clear and there's nothing that could go wrong." They enter a cave not realizing they're using the wrong fin strokes. When they turn around to leave the cave, the silt on the cave floor has been stirred up and visibility is gone. It can sometimes take hours for that sediment to settle and the exit to become visible, but by then you may not have hours of air in your tank. Equine therapy can look so simple, so effortless, and in reality it's not. And that presents a danger to all of us in terms of credibility on many levels.

## Budgeting

**T**he next big scary thing for many people is the budget process. And, like your business plan, it's an important and crucial element to running things successfully.

Your initial budget will come from your Business Plan, and then be further developed into specific details.

At its heart, a budget consists of two main elements: income and expenses. It then allocates where you will derive that income, and where the expenses will be spent. If you begin to see disparity between income and expenses, it can be your first clue that something is not right with your business model. It can help you understand where the bulk of your money is going, and if the ratios between them are correct. Are you billing correctly? Are you consistently underestimating costs?

## Income: **The First Half** of the Budgeting Equation

**O**ur core business at *Horse Sense* is individual outpatient psychotherapy, helping people build mental health and life skills by working with horses. In 2006, we averaged about 20 individual sessions per week, about half of which were JCPC and contract clients, and half of which were Medicaid clients. The reality right now is that this preponderance of low-income clients doesn't allow us make a living;

## Income, General

| Type of Income | Amount | # of Sessions, @ $100/session |
|---|---|---|
| 20% Private Pay (cash, CC) | $25,320 | 3 sessions/week for 50 weeks |
| 35% Insurance, Medicaid, Medicare | $44,310 | 5-6 sessions/week for 50 weeks |
| 30% Grants | $37,980 | 5 sessions/week for 50 weeks |
| 15% Fundraising & Scholarship/Sponsorship | $18,990 | $938/month |

**Total of 22 sessions/week for 50 weeks**
(Projected Income is equal to Expenses on page 48)

**Total**  **$126,600**

we can't generate the income we need to cover payroll. However, the situation is a whole lot better now than it was, and we're beginning to balance out our low-income client population with clients and groups who *can* pay full rate for our services. Although we will never stop seeing low-income and Medicaid clients, we need balance to support the financial health of the business. We've learned that the hard way.

It takes time to grow your business and establish your customer base . . . which is the overwhelming reason you need capital to fund that growth period. In addition to that there's often a lag time with payment, and you've got to have capital to cover turnaround time for both grant money and insurance claims. The more clients you develop as private pay the better off your financial health will be.

I recommend growing your business by working part-time to start with, and easing toward full-time as you transition, getting your name out in the community. Develop "currency and fluency" in your community—defining who you are and what you do. Taking the slow route lets you start building gradually, getting a better idea of how easy or how hard it is going to be to transition into full-time. You have to support your business. You have a facility to maintain. You have horses that need to eat, get vet care and have their feet trimmed.

## Setting **Rates**

**T**he first part of determining your income level is setting your rates and determining what to charge for your services. Many businesses lack confidence in setting their fees. I had this fear that people would assume we were too expensive to afford, because of the horses and the facilities. And I also assumed we didn't have the credibility because we didn't have the statistics. So I started out bending over backwards to make it credible, and to show we were affordable. Right away, not charging what I needed to make became a real problem. I believed in the process but undervalued our services due to lack of confidence in demand. I had to learn to believe we had value, and that we had a right to ask for that value. I think this is fairly common phenomenon in new business, no matter what the specialty. People have a hard time acknowledging the worth of their product, and in the beginning they are always loathe to turn clients away. We were the same.

Determining your rate begins with doing homework to find out what your competition's going rate is. Compare yourself to similar services, whether it be psychotherapy, adult learning, or adventure team building. Use that as a starting point for developing your pricing structure, and then tweak it to fit other business factors like number of billable team hours, costs, etc. In the beginning, I priced sessions by assuming two hours of staff time for every one hour with clients. I would tack on $10-12 per hour more to handle overhead, everything else from insurance, to horses, to farm rental, etc. Even with this, we started out pricing low. Become business savvy and know the going rates in your area. Lanier Cordell says it well in her excellent book *Equinomics: the Secret to Making Money with Your Horse Business*: charge what you need to make.

If clients went to someone else for psychotherapy, who would they go to, and how much would they pay per hour for that service? I find our rates at *Horse Sense* are comparable to that of an office therapist. Our rates started out too low, but then we readjusted when we saw both the amount of time required and effectiveness our clients received. You may find, as we did, that our clients received extremely effective therapy in fewer sessions with EAP than with a traditional therapist or through traditional therapy alone. Factor in also the fact that an EAP team consists of three units—therapist, ES, and horse—instead of one person in a traditional office therapy session, and you begin to see the justification in pricing.

We now price ourselves in the same range as an office therapist. Our average session is $120 per hour, and our intake session is priced at $140, with one and one half to two hours for pre- and post-testing.

Many young programs set rates based on paying their therapists and equine specialists on a per-session rate, which is the most effective way to price in the beginning. If I were to do that now, I would probably set an hourly rate and then divide it 40/40/20 or 45/45/10 between the therapist, the ES, and barn/business overhead.

## The **Sliding Scale Fee** & How it Affects Income

**I**n some ways, I still very much tend to operate more like a non-profit than a **for-profit.** Implementing a sliding scale fee was an important part of our program. While being a for-profit organization, we wanted to make sure that room was always left for those who could not afford to pay; we wouldn't turn away people in need because of limited resources.

In the beginning, our lowest sliding scale fee from was $5, based on an annual income of less than $15,000. We've since modified these numbers and the cutoff scale to fit more appropriately. However, having this capability also means that other parts of the budget need to make up for the income we lose helping these clients. The sliding scale fee helped us, in terms of serving everyone we wanted to serve, and we continue to implement it today. But if you're going to utilize it, some other funding mechanism needs to be in place.

We've developed alternate sources of funding to compensate. We now have a scholarship fund to help people who have few resources. We apply for grant money in cooperation with other non-profits. And we are trying to increase the numbers of full-pay clients so their fees help take pressure off costs.

If people want to donate money to our program, they can contribute to the *Horse Sense* scholarship fund by donating through the Mountin' Hopes non-profit therapeutic riding program . . . just one of several ways our programs combine efforts to make services more affordable to everyone.

| | $75,000 + Up | $40,000 - 74,999 | Up to $39,999 |
|---|---|---|---|
| Initial Assessment (80 min.) | $140 | $120 | $100 |
| Individual, Duo & Family (50 min.) | 120 | 95 | 80 |
| Individual, Duo & Family (80 min.) | 210 | 180 | 150 |

## Income Through **Grant Money**

**E**ven as for-profit, *Horse Sense* **started collaborating with a non-profit almost immediately.** At the end of 2003, there was a notice in the paper that the Juvenile Crime and Prevention Council (JCPC) was allocating funds for programs specializing in at-risk youth, one of our target populations at *Horse Sense*. So I wrote a grant.

I had many people try to discourage me with, "Don't work too hard, you're not going to get this." I ignored their advice. I wrote a grant to the best of my ability, was very excited about it, pitched it to the council (a room full people who had no idea who we were), and to our amazement . . . got the grant.

But there was an immediate problem. The grant required *Horse Sense* to be either a public or a non-profit program, which we found out at our first meeting with the agency. We were neither. Alarm bells began going off, and our one and only grant nearly died on the spot. One thing saved the day: our association with an equine non-profit group (no longer in existence). Through our relationship to this program, we were able to arrange to have them act as our fiscal agent, with their board of directors overseeing our program. We set up a contract with them for our services, and our program was able to provide its therapy to these youth.

With this experience under our belt, we were able to move forward to create a new alliance with Mountin' Hopes, a therapeutic riding facility just down the road and closer to our neck of the woods. We have since worked together on several successful grant projects, our joint work providing access to therapy for dozens of juvenile justice clients. With JCPC grants, for example, we do all the footwork to write the grants, and Mountin' Hopes oversees the fiscal matters and receives some compensation for their effort and expense involved with coordinating the services. Mountin' Hopes does not serve juvenile justice kids on their property and does not provide mental health services, so the grant is an ideal partnership for us both.

With Mountin' Hopes, we now have different contractual arrangements for different programs. We may be co-creators and co-writers of a grant or we may provide peripheral services under a grant that is solely theirs. We negotiate these programs on an case-by-case basis. We also do the occasional joint fundraising effort, again splitting out funds based on manpower, effort, and time.

## Compensation, Insurance, and "Super Billing"

**B**illing and compensation can be one of the most challenging areas of income flow for a business—just ask any medical office.

One of the first things you need to be aware of is that if you are conducting business as a mental health organization, you definitely want the LPC or LCSW licensure. When *Horse Sense* first started out, our therapist did not have an LPC designation, so we couldn't bill Medicaid or insurance.

Even when we had therapists with the proper designation to bill, we still had a mountain of paperwork to plow through, paperwork I frankly didn't understand. After a search, we found someone who handles insurance claims processing and filing. This member of our virtual team tells us what we need to collect to bill, and takes a certain percentage out of every claim filed. If we don't collect, she doesn't collect. We use the same codes as the traditional medical community for filing insurance claims. My philosophy for using an outside processing party was the same as my philosophy for using an outside bookkeeper: I knew we could get into big trouble messing up insurance filing, and I wanted to have it done as professionally as possible without the burden of insurance filing on top of our other paperwork.

If you outsource your claims processing, I recommend searching for a processing provider used to working with non-traditional service providers such as chiropractors and "play therapy" programs. Talk to local chiropractors and therapy programs to find out who they use. It's helpful to find someone accustomed to dealing with non-traditional services like ours, in case they have to go to bat with the insurance company. We also found it extremely helpful hiring a therapist who had run their own practice. They often already know all of this, and might be able to help direct your business through the maze.

Even with this service in place, insurance filing is a complicated and time-consuming process. The insurance company doesn't give a hoot about pleasing us as an organization; they only care about pleasing their client, your client. If the client utilizes services and wants to file a claim for insurance, you are the one taking the gamble on getting paid. If insurance denies you, you still have to get paid. In the meantime, months may have passed since the original service, all without compensation.

So we are now in the process of getting out of insurance billing, and switching to a concept called "super billing," otherwise known as "fee slip" or "patient filing." Super billing gets us out from between the insurance company and the client. We expect payment at the time of service, and provide the client with the paperwork necessary for submitting the insurance claim themselves.

The bottom line is that insurance companies don't care what we think, they care what the client thinks. We've had clients who have written letters to request payment from their insurance companies, with far better results. The insurance company will listen to the client long before us.

Of course the great issue we're speaking about here is that of credibility again. Insurance companies are only now becoming aware of this new form of therapy, and the burden of fighting for claim payment as a non-traditional service is tremendous. We've had insurance companies cover our services on an arbitrary basis. We're at the whims of the insurance company and that's not a good place to be if you want to stay alive. It's only one part of the battle the EAP field is fighting in the effort to become recognized by traditional doctors, therapists, government agencies, and insurance organizations.

I want to highlight the importance of incorporating pre- and post-testing into your sessions. Numbers translate into legitimacy. With mental health providers closing their doors and increased competition for funding, our industry, as a newer form of therapy, needs to accumulate statistics that establish our effectiveness as a therapy. The biggest barrier to charging what we're worth—whether in the form of cash, insurance coverage, *or* securing grant money—is credibility. Ideally, everyone doing equine assisted practice should be doing their part to accumulate and contribute to research so we can build a body of statistical evidence to prove our effectiveness. The more we all do this, the better off we all are.

## Turning **Success into Fair Rates**

**I**recommend you utilize super billing from the outset for your program. Paperwork and procedures for handling insurance filing costs medical offices thousands of dollars each year. While *Horse Sense* still currently accepts Medicaid, the paperwork is overwhelming, even if we're not filing it ourselves.

## **Expenses: The Second Half** of the Budgeting Equation

**P**rogram costs and expenditures form the other side of your budget formula, and work against income to produce either your profit or deficit. Big expense categories for equine assisted practice include salary, taxes, insurance (health, property, liability, etc), administrative costs (phones, copiers, computers), and facility (horse care, maintenance, equipment).

As we've said before, equine assisted practice has a lot of moving parts . . . expensive, high-maintenance moving parts. Those of you in the equine industries know that horse-related businesses often fail under the burden of big-ticket items like barns, arenas, heavy equipment, horse purchases, horse care, and liability insurance. In equine

## Expenses, General

| Type of Expense | Annual |
|---|---|
| Salary/Wages and Taxes for 1 full-time ES and 1 full-time Therapist | 70,000 (40,000 for Therapist; 30,000 for ES) $8,000 for taxes = $78,000 |
| Insurance (Farm Liability, Program Liability Professional Liability) | $5,000 (ballpark for all insurances) |
| Professional Services (accounting, graphic and website design, biz cards, etc.) | $15,000 (depending on which services utilized) |
| Office Supplies and Such (printer rental, port-a-jon, printing, phones, utility, credit card charges, etc.) | $5,000 |
| Horses and Facilities (4 horses, 1 outdoor and 1 indoor facility, renting, not building) | $12,000 |
| Education and Training | $1,000 (attending an annual conference, other workshops, mentoring/supervision, etc.) |
| Travel & Lodging (for Education, etc.) | $600 (depending on where you go and where you stay!) |
| **Total** | **$116,600** |

assisted programs, you can add the costs of trained therapists and equine specialists to that mix which loads down expenses even more. Careful calibration of these expenses against income is a big part of maintaining equilibrium. I won't go into specific numbers, accounting principles, or financial management here. But know that, like other aspects of EAP and EAL, managing expenses requires careful monitoring and common sense.

Facility and horse care expenses for *Horse Sense* are greatly simplified due to the leasing arrangement it has with Meadows Town, LLC. These costs are wrapped into a single fixed expense at the end of the month

**UN-**DESPAIR

September 10, 2004

Shannon Knapp
Horse Sense of the Carolinas, Inc.
Marshall, NC

Dear Shannon,

I am writing in support of your grant application to the WNC Community Foundation for the Family Sense program. It is my understanding that the Family Sense program will provide Equine Assisted Psychotherapy and Therapeutic Riding for identified families, with the goal of strengthening the family unit.

Women At Risk is an outpatient mental health and substance abuse treatment program for women who are at risk of going to jail or prison. We have had contact with Horse Sense through a staff demonstration and an all-day workshop for Women At Risk clients. I am continually impressed with the level of skill and care provided by Horse Sense staff when working with clients. The service they provide is unique and powerful. Our collaboration to provide the all-day workshop for Women At Risk clients was so beneficial, we have already started planning to offer this again in the fall.

Many of our clients belong to families with an identified "special needs" member. I believe the Horse Sense staff is prepared to deal with this population. I think that families would benefit from the Family Sense program as individual family members learn about themselves and each other, address the structure and functioning of the family unit, and increase effective communication and conflict resolution skills.

I am delighted to offer support for this application. Please contact me if I can provide any additional information.

Sincerely,

Brenda Carleton, MSW, LCSW, CCAS, CCS
Program Director

*A letter written in support of Horse Sense as we applied for a local grant.*

paid as rent. If your program owns and manages its facility, this line item becomes quite a bit more complicated. Feed, veterinary and farrier costs, worming, vaccinations, fencing, fuel, and equipment all play into this number and represent a wide range of variables to control that tie directly to your experience and skill as an agriculture and facility manager.

Staffing is another major expense issue for *Horse Sense* where management expertise—especially in hiring and negotiating salaries—plays a big part in controlling costs. In its early stages we had too much staff, which in turn put too much pressure on overhead costs. The decision to staff *Horse Sense* with full-time therapists and ES's, rather than starting out part-time, came from the desire to meet other objectives, which we'll discuss in future chapters. But it was definitely a trade-off, and a huge burden to the business up front. If I had to do it over again I would have kept my staff in part time jobs somewhere else, and for a longer period, than I did before I put them on full time at *Horse Sense*. Adding or cutting staff is a real vulnerable point of transition when growing your business.

When it comes to other big-ticket expense categories, like insurance and office equipment, the standard "buyer beware" warning applies. Always take the time to shop around and get multiple quotes on items like phone systems, copier rentals, and insurance policies. Striking variations in pricing and service will reveal themselves; you can easily overspend if you're not careful. Beware of long-term equipment contracts as the need for more serious machines becomes necessary. Rental contracts for office equipment, telephone service, high-speed Internet, cell phones, and maintenance services can cost thousands of dollars if negotiated improperly. Contracts of this nature can be a red flag item for trouble in any business.

It should go without saying that a good bookkeeper was the first resource *Horse Sense* hired when it opened; tax issues, too, were put straight into the hands of an expert. But remember: just because you utilize financial people doesn't get you off the hook for knowing, understanding, and staying involved in the financial management of your business . . . or writing your budget!

## Systems for **Daily Business**

**I**n the beginning, the systems in place to run *Horse Sense* could be summed up in three words: we winged it. With a staff of three people (one therapist, one full-time equine specialist, and myself) there just wasn't much to manage at first.

We had my computer and a printer. We had business cards. We had a phone number, and the phone . . . well, actually the phone was my cell phone. That was it. We didn't have many systems in place, and even though we were in a state of flux, more structure and more planning certainly would have been helpful, even if that "something" was itself fairly makeshift. As the situation quickly began to change, having something weak would have been better than nothing at all. Our policies, both in the barn and in the office, were drawn up on the fly, sometimes to the detriment of our time and energy.

Here are some office policies and systems I'd recommend before you start doing business:

* Draw up a simple Standard Operating Procedures (SOP) manual. It doesn't have to be detailed, just begin putting basic procedures down in writing: answering the phone, scheduling sessions, emergency phone numbers, and staff contact information. Think about the different situations your staff may face, then find solutions and write them out.

* Have forms for tracking phone calls and queries. As I said before, it would be so helpful now to look back and see how many people called, where they were from, how they heard about us, and what questions they usually asked.

* After developing your forms, it's probably a good idea to review them on a regular basis. If something isn't relevant to your system, clean it out.

* In EAP, as with other forms of therapy, client confidentiality, and security of client paperwork is critical. Employee documentation is also highly confidential. For that reason, you will need some sort of charting and filing system for clients and employees, kept in locked, fireproof storage in a locked office. This double lock system is important for all confidential files in your offices. There are various requirements about how long you should keep files, and you should probably refer to your professional licensing organization, your accountant, and regulations specific to your situation. I keep files for up to seven years post treatment. Keep any computer program you use for tracking data locked up and secure so information is protected.

## Forms and Paperwork

**E**very business needs a variety of forms to keep processes, procedures, and **systems on track.** At the same time, paperwork can become unwieldy and redundant. Start by looking at policies from other programs. You can find *Horse Sense's* paperwork by visiting our website and logging in to the *Horse Sense Business Sense* member's section.

At my first EAGALA conference in San Diego, I bought as many books and manuals from other people as were available. Some of these had programs and activities, others included paperwork and form templates as well. Susan Taylor's website (equine-psychotherapy.org) is another place to look, offering materials online for everyone to examine and use. We started with her templates for paperwork and forms, and adapted them to *Horse Sense* versions, then constantly modified them until they were a perfect fit. It would be interesting to put our paperwork now beside Susan's today and see if any of it is still the same!

Here's a list of the crucial forms you need to have prior to seeing your first client:

* **Psychological Evaluation/intake:** A formal Psychological Evaluation form is necessary, especially if you are doing mental health. Our first assessment form was huge, nearly 20 pages long, and overkill for our use. We quickly adapted to a slimmed-down version that helped us capture the information we needed.

* **Registration Form:** This form collects all the basic client information, including billing and insurance information, if applicable. This form includes our "Consent to Treat for Therapy" client or guardian signature line.

* **Policies and procedures document**, including the map of the facilities and HIPPA information (see page 63 for map).

* **Equine Liability:** When we first started we drew up a liability agreement with help from a lawyer who specialized in equine law. We found him through the North Carolina Horse Council. Even though these forms can be found in most of the horse books out there, and most states do have an official equine liability statement for businesses, I recommend following up with a qualified attorney and verifying the current rules and conditions. In the barn itself, we post the North Carolina Equine Statute, as required.

* **A Referral Form**, to be filled out for us by the primary therapist, physician, or other involved party.

* **Release of Information Consent form**, for permission to discuss, as appropriate, the client with another treatment team member, such as the primary therapist.

* **Medical History Form**, to be completed by the client or parent/guardian.

* **Important Emergency Info Form**, which includes current medications taken, and permission to treat (or not) in case of accident or injury.

* **A Treatment Goals form** and **Discharge Form**.

* **Progress Notes Form**: Progress notes need to be kept in each client file, on paper

or on computer. Make sure your form covers everything necessary for therapists to record, including any insurance codes or information. There has been some discussion whether notes on the horses should be part of progress notes themselves. At *Horse Sense*, they are not. Therapists document each session, but the activities or horses aren't named. As in other forms of experiential therapy, the actual specifics of each activity are not spelled out . . . it's just too much detail.

✳ **Pre/Post Testing Instruments**: Paperwork needs to be in place for anything that needs to be recorded. Pre- and post-testing forms are very important in our field. The "Y-OQ®" or Youth Outcome Questionnaire is one such tool we use because it has a youth self-report and a parent report contained in the form. We use them for pre-, mid-, and post-session information gathering. These can reveal extremely important information from the client and parents involved, and collecting such data helps us in the field to develop statistically significant results.

✳ Your therapist may need to have a **professional disclosure statement** as part of the paperwork a client signs. In North Carolina for example, an LPC must present this document at the start of treatment.

A variety of other forms that we've developed over the years can be found on our website. Some forms that have been phased out do not appear, such as the Safety Contract. While we've dropped that form for client work, we still use it for our general horse activities and public events such as traditional horse clinics.

## More about the **Safety Contract**

**O**ur original "Safety Contract" was a document reviewed and signed by each client at the start of their first session with the horses. It covered the barn rules and a lot of basic things about being around horses. We ended up reconsidering the issue of a Safety Contract after realizing we could talk endlessly about safety, horses, and "how-to" information (how to hold the rope, how to move around the horse) and never, ever capture it all. Learning about working around horses is a *lifelong* process.

Instead, we've made it part of the awareness process that EAP & EAL offers clients.

Clients quickly realize the detrimental consequences of wearing flip-flops to a barn. They become alert and receptive to learning how a horse moves and thinks, and thinking through that process itself serves to engage them more fully in their sessions.

A lot of safety issues can become overkill, driven I think primarily by our own fears. It's true that horses require much in regard to safety and awareness, but we found it important to distinguish between that and a reactionary mindset. We used the Safety Contract for a year or so, and it made us feel better. But I don't know what kind of difference it made for the clients. As David Currie of Classic Equestrian Assisted Family Services says at the beginning of every session (and we do, too), "Horses are always looking out for their own safety. How about you?"

## Human Resources


**A**lthough we'll be covering staffing and building a team in Chapter Five, I want to discuss a few basic procedures and policies as they relate to the function of Human Resources staffing. The HR function in any company is an issue to take seriously. Hiring and management practices are an important issue whether you operate as a non-profit or for-profit organization. Businesses can get into plenty of trouble managing this function poorly.

If you're a part-time, backyard program, your HR needs are going to be pretty simple. However, if you have a more extensive program and aren't especially knowledgeable about Human Resources, you might want to consider adding the services of an HR consultant to your Virtual Team. Consultants are responsible for knowing the latest laws and regulations, and can provide a wealth of information on best practices for finding, interviewing, and hiring employees. They can also help you prepare for the more serious task of managing employees after the hire: developing an HR Manual, processes for disciplinary action, etc.

*Horse Sense* utilizes the standard Human Resources procedures: Equal Opportunity and Workman's Comp policies, with information posted in employee break rooms. We have a health insurance plan in place. A retirement plan is waiting in the wings, once the business becomes more viable. I utilized referrals from my accountant and word-of-mouth to find agents and brokers for insurances quotes, and I strongly suggest getting multiple quotes from several agents so that you can find the best plans possible.

We paid the *Horse Sense* staff by the hour when we started, a decision that, while not being the best business move, was still the right thing to do for the employees. I decided not to follow the concept of paying therapists and ES's per session; I wanted to have staff on hand and ready when people called for an appointment. I also wanted to begin the team-building process right away, rather than wait for there to be enough business to justify the cost. We had a lot to learn, and a long way to go before we operated as a cohesive unit. I didn't want to spend our initial months operating in a void with nothing in place to build the team. There was probably a wiser way to start out, but keeping the staff intact and in tune was my focus.

Retaining employees and knowing what keeps an employee healthy for work in this business is a balance I always watch for. In looking at hiring procedures, I'd probably start with a lower salary, and plan to provide more in the form of bonuses and rewards. Research shows that pay is less of a motivator in keeping a happy employee than feeling valued and getting regular feedback. We strive to help each employee develop their special interest in EAP. We have one ES who keeps her focus on eating disorders, another employee whose interest is in high-risk and at-risk youth, and another who is developing an interest in training medical professionals.

Initially, we didn't do annual reviews, since our early business was very small and informal. However, the value of an annual review procedure became apparent as we started adding staff. When we first began doing annual reviews, we went to the nearest office supply store, got the performance evaluation packet, and used their forms. We conduct the review by holding a meeting. I fill out a sheet on the employee, the employee fills out a sheet on themselves, and we spend some time reviewing it. We then go through the same procedure to evaluate my performance. We each sign off on the forms and all copies go into the employee's folder. So now employees have some clear guidelines, ideas where they're going, and a plan. We've become a lot more specific.

## Our Policy for **Internships & Volunteers**

**Y**our business is going to get plenty of calls from volunteers, mostly people who want to work around horses. The horse stuff is the easy part, the part everybody wants to volunteer for. However, equine assisted therapy doesn't utilize volunteers in the same way as a therapeutic riding organization, which needs plenty of volunteer bodies to work with multiple horses and sometimes multiple clients in one session.

At *Horse Sense* we made it clear from the outset that we didn't have a volunteer program, due in large part to confidentiality issues. Volunteer positions are often too flimsy for my comfort, and usually require a lot of management. Today if someone calls wanting horse time, we refer them to the horse rescue or therapeutic riding programs down the road.

Internships, on the other hand, are ideal, and *Horse Sense* has worked with some very fun and exciting people through its internship program. We have an increased level of commitment and dedication when we work with interns vs. volunteers, and we can control the scheduling and exposure to clients. Many interns are there as part of a learning experience, under supervision from an overseeing institution and guided by a curriculum for attaining knowledge. We specifically seek people interested in developing skills for EAP and EAL. And we've had some terrific interns who've really stuck. We now host one to two unpaid interns per semester and, with the exception of therapy sessions themselves, they're exposed to a little bit of everything that we do. Depending on the kind of internship, client contact hours will be incorporated as well.

If you decide to take on volunteers and interns, be aware that obligations in this area need to be taken seriously. People need to be processed into the system, monitored, and evaluated, just like an employee. It is possible that issues regarding safety, training, and confidentiality could crop up and come back to bite the program. For that reason, I advocate very strong, clear procedures for taking on interns and volunteers. Be clear about their scope of work. And be prepared for them to take as much work as an employee.

## Meetings

**A** big part of managing our team comes in the form of structured meetings. Once your organization grows beyond two people, it becomes important to create forums for regular communication.

Here's a list of the *Horse Sense* meetings when we first started out:

✳ Weekly core team meeting for full-time staff

* Weekly clinical meetings for therapists and for specific case studies. This meeting follows the Core meeting each week.

* ES meetings

Our core meetings today are shorter, with an agenda that incorporates aspects from the full "menu" of meetings we used to have. The clinical meeting now rotates between mock sessions, clinical reviews, and in-house education.

## Scheduling

Scheduling wasn't so much of a problem when the program only had one therapist. There wasn't a chance an ES was going to be booked with something else, unless it was me going to grant meetings or a networking event. Our ES was pretty much always available. Because we were seeing a lot of after-school kids, our hours tended to differ from a traditional doctor's office. We found 10AM–6PM worked for us, and planned on a 4-day work week Wednesday through Saturday.

Scheduling became tricky once we had more than one therapist, and the need for an administrative person also became clear . . . especially when it came to developing a calendar. When six people were inputting items into the calendar, we had numerous screw-ups and scheduling conflicts. Having one person handling the schedule virtually eliminated those errors.

We now have a couple of systems that help us keep track: a color-coded system (on the Macintosh iCal calendar program) keeps everyone's schedule straight, and can be printed out. Magnets on a dry-erase board list all the activities of the week with client initials, times, and team assignments. So far we haven't experienced the need to develop a system more complex than this, but then again our team works within one office and is close at hand. Other programs may find the need to develop more sophistication.

## Recommended **Reading**

*E-Myth Revisited*, Michael Gerber

*Equine Assisted Psychotherapy Business Planning Guide & Workbook*, Barbara J. Scott

*The One Page Business Plan*, Jim Horan

# Chapter FOUR

## Building a **Facility:** MY **STORY** continued

*I had been coming to the Asheville area since I was a little girl. My husband and I got married here in 1996.* *After years living in Dallas, we knew we wanted to move to Asheville and build a farm so that our rescue and rehabilitation work with dogs could be expanded to working with horses. We came here looking for fifty acres and a place to call home.*

*It took about two years to find. We started in 1998 by renting a little one-bedroom apartment in Asheville. We began commuting between Asheville and Dallas, spending long weekends and vacations looking for property and spending time with the realtor between outings of kayaking and hiking.*

*We wanted the property to be accessible to Asheville while still having plenty of acreage—about three acres per horse—to accommodate a reasonable number of rescue animals.*

*Finding land was easy; finding usable land was another matter entirely. Property suitable for horses meant finding moderately level ground in the mountains. We knew that only time and patience would turn up the right location. We finally found it in 2000: an old family cattle farm situated 25 miles and two big turns north of Asheville. The property had a little ranch-style brick house, two old tobacco barns, plenty of barbed wire fence, and 65 acres of hayfields and pasture. We moved in the summer of 2000, along with our horses Masada and Susan Denero (Black-eyed Sue), and went straight to work.*

*In retrospect, we would have built more slowly if we had known how the business would develop. We built way too much too soon, and as the idea for* Horse Sense *took form, the business that emerged could not keep up with the financial outlay. Our cash flow did not catch up for a long while.*

## Structures

**The beauty of EAP is that it can be done with great simplicity: a horse, a therapist, and a client.** You don't have to have an extensive facility to do equine-assisted activity in its purest form: just the basics for good horse care and a qualified team. However, remember again to always consider the Stephen Covey adage: "Begin with the end in mind."

Here again, the rationale for writing a good business plan comes into play. In our case, we began building quickly once we bought our land. Certainly it made a difference that we bought the land as part of our home, that we had our own funding, and that we were building to accommodate a horse rehabilitation farm, not an equine assisted practice. No doubt it would have been extremely beneficial to have had a five-year plan in place, and to plan the build-out of our property to coincide with the income from a developing business . . . or even to know that it would be a certain number of years before the business would catch up with our building process.

Instead, as the vision for our business changed, we ended up creating a lot of make-do arrangements rather than following a master plan. When you piece together an operation, inevitably parts of it then have to be partially dismantled and rebuilt. Great potential exists for spending money where and when you shouldn't, and many times money has to be spent again to do it right. It's not a practical way to do business.

59

## Things **Horses Need**

**T**he biggest consideration for an equine business is, of course, providing for the horses themselves.** And those considerations include the basics of food, shelter, and adequate care for both the mental and physical comfort of the animals. From a business perspective, Meadows Town, LLC officially handles the herd's care and upkeep, including feeding, equipment, and vet and farrier care. When we first started, Meadows Town used to bring the horses to and from the arena every day as well . . . a process that became way too cumbersome to handle, especially since Meadows Town in essence consisted of one person—my husband—and the additional formality was overkill.

Like many EAGALA practitioners, *Horse Sense* believes in keeping horses in an environment that is as natural as possible. We follow the theory that the single greatest gift horses give us in EAP/EAL is their natural instincts . . . so the more we do provide a natural environment, the more intact those natural instincts will be. The more artificial the environment, the more we block what makes equine assisted practice so unique.

Given that horses today have been removed from the wild and the natural rhythms of herd life, we strive to keep our horses on full-time pasture board at *Horse Sense*, along with as much natural shelter in the form of windbreaks as possible. Horses are sub-arctic animals, designed to survive in an environment where they can move about freely. Except for the most extreme kinds of weather, a horse can regulate and maintain their body heat much better in pasture conditions than they can in a stall. Our horses aren't kept in stalls unless they're in a rehabilitation or recovery situation. At the height of summer we might have a couple of horses in for the day, especially those sensitive to the bugs and heat, to give them some relief and a little "day spa" quality time.

Another thing a horse needs is other horses. Again, everything in the horse's psychological makeup is geared towards living in a herd environment, so the more natural we can make it, the better. We have several small pastures where we group our horses two to four at a time. We rotate the horses from pasture to pasture, keeping the mares separate from the geldings to make things easier. Once or twice a year, we might turn all the geldings out in the hayfield together after the last cutting.

A regular schedule of veterinary care, farrier visits, and a program of good nutrition completes the regimen. Our horses are barefoot unless they need to be otherwise. If there's a reason for shoeing, then by all means they are shod. There's no particular school we subscribe to in terms of hoof care; it's addressed on a case-by-case basis for each horse. We feed our horses hay and grain with vitamin and mineral supplements by Advanced Biological Concepts (A-B-C-Plus. com).

These things, of course, are only the basics. There are literally hundreds of resources, books, theories, and schools of thought pertaining to horse care, accompanied by hundreds of equally varying opinions. The one thing I think most horse people agree on

**UN-DESPAIR**

change
Change
change in me,
i stand in the round pen
tall yet very small
claiming my space to stay safe
i'm not alone in this place
only i can keep it safe
he enters bumps,pushes and even nibbles
it's rude and scary
frozen in the past and feeling in the present
he comes real close--change
i risk it all to stand tall.
i push him away safe and all.
change in me
i can be free.

written by p.s.
dedicated to scout
12/12/03

One of our very first clients, this poem was written for Scout, the appaloosa who appears on the back cover of this book.

is this: you need to know what you're doing when it comes to horse care. And non-horse people new to the field of equine management can get themselves in a world of trouble trying to take care of horses, from providing for their own personal safety to understanding all there is to know about horses themselves. Since this book isn't designed to teach you about caring for horses, please make sure you have studied and learned everything you can before you begin, and continue to learn as you go. The references and books that I hold in highest regard are listed at the end of this chapter.

## Necessary vs. **Nice**

**N**ow that we've considered the horses, we can consider the needs of the business itself. When it comes to building the facility for your equine assisted program, there are two lists you can compile: a list of the things you *should* have to do this work, and a list of things that are *nice* to have.

So let's assume you have the following: a treatment team (an ES and a therapist), 3-5 happy, healthy horses, a pasture, halter, and lead rope. Of course you will have storage needs for hay and grain. Storage should be both rodent- and horse-proof, with sealed containers for grain. Keep feed materials in a dry, covered area. And again, be sure it's well out of reach from your horses! You'll also need a telephone, a locking fireproof file cabinet kept in a secure space within a locked room, and a computer with a printer. The computer will help you generate all the forms you need. The physical pieces are in place. So now let's move on to things that are *nice* to have to fill out your business, but not entirely necessary.

Although good to have, it amazes some people that you don't need a building to do equine assisted work. In fact, at *Horse Sense* we conduct as many sessions as possible out in pasture. A enclosed space of 50-foot x 80-foot is ideal, for starters. An arena is nice to have, a lighted arena is even nicer! *Horse Sense* has a barn with these amenities that can be used as a fallback facility for bad weather. Having a roof, lighting, and an place to work is tremendously helpful and reduces dependency on good weather and daylight hours. Our indoor facility also comes into play working with high-risk youth. We usually don't start an adjudicated youth, or any client with a high flight risk, out in pasture. So having an indoor, secure facility is helpful until the client can work up to an open situation.

It's nice to have all sorts of different props for EAP and EAL work: cones, jumps, PVC poles, hula hoops, foam noodles, big balls. You'll need a place to keep all the props, even if it's the sides and the corners of the arena, to keep items out of the way. Chairs are nice for larger groups, especially those designed to be stacked and stored between sessions. Basic equipment for maintaining the arena should include a wheelbarrow for transporting stuff (including manure), a pitchfork, and a rake or harrow. We also keep spare boots, gloves, and jackets on hand for clients during cold weather.

An office space for the team is another nice item for your list, a place where client assessments can take place. A separate phone line, a copier, and other office equipment become very helpful as the team grows.

## Building **the Buildings**

**K**eep in mind that amenities like a barn, an arena, and other structures are nice things to have, not strict necessities. However, when you're ready to begin developing and building some serious structures, remember Pat Parelli's saying: "Take the time it takes, and it'll take less time." When it comes to building out your facility, know that if you skimp on some things in the beginning you may end up with more work in the end. Build the right facility once so you don't have to keep rebuilding over and over.

While we did a lot of things right in building our farm, we also made plenty of mistakes at *Horse Sense*. For example, if I could do it over, I would make the initial arena as big as I could get away with. I'd plan to have a bathroom in the tack room area, rather than adding it later. I'd have an office and classroom closer to the main session area.

My advice: get plenty of advice from those around you! I had the benefit of advice from those in the area, people who had better ideas. I thought I had good ideas for the arena and barns, but inevitably someone more experienced would come over and give me a host of better ideas. Consult with others who have built barns and arenas, and those who've developed acreages. People who've "been there, done that" can be tremendously helpful pointing out trouble spots—like poor drainage—or giving you things to consider. Ask a lot of questions: why did you do it this way, why not that way? What would you do differently? Not only are many people happy to share their experiences, it becomes tremendously helpful to develop a network of knowledgeable contacts and neighbors.

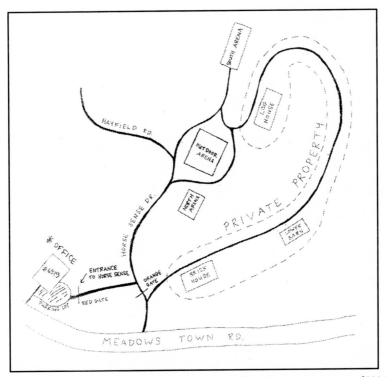

*The Horse Sense map of our property given to clients. This reflects our property as of 2004.*

Find builders and contractors who give free consultations, then get their feedback on things like building placement and orientation, drainage, dirt moving, well-digging, electrical, and fencing. You will not only find a wide variety of opinions (and certainly some questionable advice), but some very valuable thoughts to consider before you begin. Learn from other people's mistakes, learn which contractors are the most knowledgeable (and respectful), and who and what to avoid.

Before you begin any serious building or development, *always* secure a range of bids from contractors. Develop a detailed budget, and map out the most realistic and ideal schedule possible. You don't want to begin a project only to learn that you'll be moving dirt during the muddy season or trying to lay underground utilities when ground is frozen in mid-winter.

We built our first two barns at *Horse Sense* in July and August 2000. We built the lower "rehabilitation" barn first (see map above), followed by the lower hay barn (not shown on map but next to lower barn), where we store and prepare all of our feed, grains, and minerals for the horses. We built the rehab barn for our rescue and rehabilitation horse work, knowing that there would be times these horses would need stall rest. Some might require separation as they go through the re-feeding process or any kind of special care. However, we didn't want to isolate them from the herd. An important part of rehabilitation is integrating the rehab horse with a natural herd environment as soon as possible. For that reason, our rehab barn is located in the center of the pasture. A horse on stall rest can be kept confined while still being among other horses to touch noses; they aren't completely isolated, reducing stress and anxiety.

The rehab barn contains four 12' x 12' stalls, with an 8' covered aisle outside the stalls and a 20' x 20' sheltered hay area on one end. With Dutch doors on the back of the stalls and sliding doors on the front, the whole structure can be opened to promote air circulation or closed down as needed. A 10' x 10' tack area is built into the other end for storage (Illustration 1).

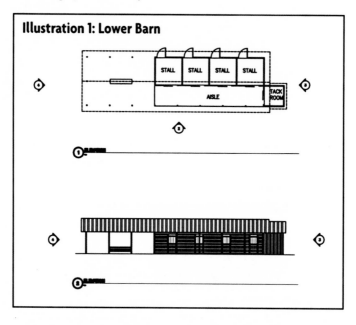

**Illustration 1: Lower Barn**

In 2001 we built the indoor arena, an indoor 60' x 120' space with six stalls on one side and a 30' x 60' storage enclosure on another side. We use cattle panels that allow us to section off up to one-third of the arena, giving us tremendous flexibility for both private and group sessions. We can keep several horses loose on one side of the arena and put an audience on the other side of the panels for observation or demonstration.

When bigger audiences are in attendance, having panels to separate people and chairs from the main activity is sometimes very necessary.

The six stalls off the main arena have Dutch doors that look into the arena area. The doors can be closed off to minimize distraction or opened to allow horses to see what's going on in the arena ... an aspect that can provide some interesting opportunities for audience members and clients. It's nice to have a variety of options, depending on what kind of activity is happening. (Illustration 2)

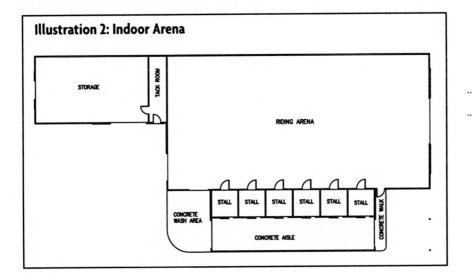

**Illustration 2: Indoor Arena**

## Arenas

**H**ere again, the number and size of formal arena space is heavily dependent on the size of your organization,** the type of work you're doing, and how extensive you want things to become.

At *Horse Sense*, we have three arenas, originally designed to give us enough capacity so that two client sessions and a horse training session could all be held at the same time ... a very ambitious plan that hasn't been cost effective as of yet because the client load hasn't been consistently realized. However, the flexibility this set up offers us is nice to have. The first arena built was the 60' x 120' indoor arena, followed by a 100' x 110' outdoor arena, and a 50' x 80' semi-enclosed covered arena with half-walls and skylight panels.

Again, there are numerous books and resources available to give you professional advice on arena build-outs, but know that drainage and footing are your primary considerations, followed by your particular requirements for all-weather use, various enclosure options, and other amenities such as lights. If you want to have a year-round program in the north, an enclosed arena is a virtual necessity, in my opinion, whereas in the South, an enclosed arena is less than ideal when considering the year-round heat and humidity. Likewise, lights are nice for winter hours and after-dark flexibility.

Proper drainage and grade are really important to developing an arena that will remain dry, level, and workable after rainfall. There's nothing more disconcerting than an arena that's not level, or an area that forms lakebeds after rain. Developing the proper footing mix, depth, and material is a science unto itself, with some barns experimenting for years before getting the mix just right. Depending on your arena configuration and local conditions (outdoor vs. indoor, high winds vs. sheltered, dry vs. moist climate) the requirements for footing can change drastically. Contractors who do nothing but equestrian arenas *do* exist . . . but typically the only way to find them is online or by networking through local barns, feed stores, and riding facilities.

After we addressed drainage, we installed recycled rubber tire footing in the *Horse Sense* arenas based on the recommendation of others and after extensive research. The material consists of rubber chopped to the consistency of mulch. Here again, there are numerous details to consider, depending on what type of rubber footing is suitable for your work. We prefer the small-piece footing due to consistency and ease of spreading. Overall the rubber footing has been excellent, providing easy maintenance, good drainage, and long wear. It's very expensive up front, but it doesn't degrade, doesn't get hot in summer, or disappear in high winds. The only problem it presents is for people with allergies to rubber, in which case we conduct sessions in pasture.

Whatever you choose for building an arena for your practice, this is one aspect of your facility where you definitely want to take the time to do extensive research and build the job right. There is nothing more worthwhile than a well-built, well-thought-out facility. A poorly-built arena, on the other hand, is a constant source of aggravation and expense.

# Additional Considerations for Facility Development

**T**he property at *Horse Sense* required a moderate amount of work before it could become suitable for our uses. There were many lessons to learn along the way, and nearly every step of property development required more of that same basic research talked about earlier. Even for those who have the benefit of growing up on a farm, research needs to be exercised on different kinds of footing, drainage, fencing, soil nutrition, heavy equipment, and basic agriculture practices. Again, I cannot emphasize enough the importance of basic research to make sure you get things right.

With the exception of our property's little brick house, which we lived in during the course of the renovations and while we were building our new home, everything on our land had to be either repaired, dismantled, or cleaned up in some form or fashion. Old buildings, including an old tobacco barn, were unsalvageable and had to be torn down. Soil testing (which I highly recommend) revealed land over-used for a single purpose and hence stripped of certain nutrients. Drainage was poor in some areas with excessive runoff in others, so dirt had to be moved and proper drainage put in.

Fencing is another area where choices are numerous and opinions are plenty. Price points, too, vary widely from the very inexpensive to the very high end. We enclosed our first pastures using Centaur HTP® fencing, an innovative product made of good, sturdy material. But while it works well for horses, we discovered it was less than ideal for hillsides and worked better on flatter land. Contractors and fencing providers can be found—once again—through checking on the Internet and networking through local barns, feed stores, and yellow pages. Consider a variety of options, while making sure you consider terrain, safety, ease of care, and budget when making choices.

We use "copperwood" split rail fencing around our outdoor arena, made from ultra-dense, treated wood grown in the high elevations of the Ozark Mountains. It's a special kind of wood, not pressure treated, but material designed for long wear so it won't fall apart as easily as traditional split rail fencing available at your local "big box" building supply store. You can find various sources carrying copperwood fencing on the Internet.

At *Horse Sense*, we fenced off the first 3-acre section at the lower barn with one confined area for turnout of horses who need restricted access to grass. This in turn opens onto a series of additional 30 acres of both hillside and flat pasture. Another area consists of hay fields where we grow our own fescue/grass hay mix.

## More About **Barn Rules**

**W**hether or not you operate with a barn/arena facility, almost all states have an equine liability declaration that needs to be posted in plain sight. The declaration is also on our liability forms which people sign. In North Carolina, facilities have to post at least two of these signs on the property.

The subject of posting barn rules and regulations has been discussed earlier in this book, but it bears further clarification here, and needs to be carefully addressed within your own organization. There have been wonderful, deep, and thoughtful discussions about this topic across the industry, with good reasoning and good arguments on both sides. At *Horse Sense*, we've made the decision not to post barn rules.

We very strongly believe that, within limits, one of the greatest tools for learning is natural consequences in action. If we post rules, we set up a series of "yes's" and "no's" and "right ways" and "wrong ways" before the client even steps foot into the session. That's not what we want to facilitate. We believe in the philosophy that the client either is responsible for or needs to develop, with assistance, his or her own sense of safety, and that interacting with the horses presents an excellent opportunity to do so.

Clients go into a session and natural consequences come into play. Those consequences, in turn, become a tool for learning some deeper truths. It's these natural outcomes that allow clients to arrive at their own conclusions and create an opportunity for learning how to think on their own while making better choices.

Some of the kids we work with have never really had to deal with the consequences of their choices; some have always been enabled to such an extent they never learn about living with consequences at all. It becomes a real problem for creating boundaries, making good choices, and adjusting to society in general. We want them to learn basic self care. For some, this may be the first time they've ever been allowed to do so. Obviously, we still look out for the client's safety. We're not going to put them with a horse that is inappropriate for them; it's our job to know our horses well enough to know what's not a good match.

## Personal Safety and **High-Risk Clients**

**O**ne question that we often hear comes in the form of regard for the safety **of our personnel (both horse and human)** and property when it comes to serving a population that includes high-risk youth. As noted earlier, *Horse Sense* does work with a lot of juvenile justice kids who have serious and potentially dangerous issues. The potential for safety risks is always in the back of our minds. *Horse Sense* is not only our business, it's also our home. Am I worried about others coming here, seeing where we live, seeing where my horses live?

We are cautious and aware of almost everything that happens on the farm, and I will say that certain concerns do occasionally manifest. Yet *Horse Sense* has turned down one client out of concern for the protection of our farm and horses. Based on this client's volatile and dangerous past, we concluded that he did indeed compromise our safety, and needed a higher level of care beyond our program capabilities. If a situation is questionable, either I or my husband act as ES in the client sessions so that we can keep a close eye on what is happening.

At the end of the day, I feel fairly philosophical about the question of safety. Long ago (and again every day!), I had to make my peace with the fact that we're never really in control. The possibility exists that clients might sometimes be upset or angry when they leave a session, and that it could pose an extra risk knowing where we live. My job is to do the job and the footwork as I see it. The rest is out of my control.

## Recommended **Reading**

*Horse Behavior & Psychology DVD Program*, Parelli

*Horsekeeping on a Small Acreage: Designing and Managing Your Equine Facility*, Cherry Hill

*Natural Horse Care*, Pat Coleby

*Natural Horse-Man-Ship*, Pat Parelli

*Stablekeeping: A Visual Guide to Safe and Healthy Horsekeeping*, Cherry Hill

*Parelli Level 1 Program*

*Revolution in Horsemanship*, Dr. Robert Miller

*Understanding the Ancient Secrets of the Horse's Mind*, Dr. Robert Miller

## Building a **Team**: MY **STORY** continued

**I**n hiring our first team member, *Horse Sense* made its first serious mistake. *We started business with a therapist who was too new in the field to have any connections in the professional world. It was a double whammy for the business; not only did no one know what the heck we did, but everyone who might refer clients to us had no idea who our therapist was. No referrals = no clients.*

*It seems such an obvious thing now, that referrals come from therapists and professionals who have a comfort level entrusting their patients with you . . . that you have the ability and, more importantly, the credibility to carry off the necessary work. The therapist's relationship in the community is crucial. Things happen far easier when the therapist has some professional relationships and connections established.*

*Because we didn't consider that singular dynamic, talking to the therapy world was a tough thing in the beginning. We had nothing to go on, and getting the respect of fellow professionals took a long, long time, and slowed us down considerably.*

## A Team **by Any Other Name . . .**

**T**he team-based structure of equine assisted practice involves a formula very different from almost every other kind of therapy. For that reason, it's important to understand the impact those differences make, not only from a therapeutic perspective, but from a business operations perspective.

When I talk about the team in equine assisted practice, I'll be talking about the EAGALA model for a facilitation team: the horse, the therapist, and the equine specialist. Though equine assisted practice has been done in a lot of ways, we'll focus on the dynamics, pitfalls, and strengths of establishing an effective team for your business based on this model. This is where the heart of our practice lives and breathes.

As I've mentioned before, a metaphor that works for me is that doing equine assisted practice is like setting a table. The therapist, the ES, and the horse are like the utensils, the napkin, and the plate at the table. The team is the place setting for the meal, *not* the meal itself. We come together and the resulting session becomes the full meal for the client. When we begin, we don't necessarily know what that meal is going to be, or how it's going to taste. We're there to facilitate and support what happens with the client.

And as such, we can get in the way pretty easily. The members of the equine assisted practice team don't make the therapy work . . . but they can certainly impair the good outcome being sought. If the team members find discussion centering too much on them, it's our clue that something is off the mark. For that reason, it's crucial to understand the importance of balancing the many dynamics of the EAP/EAL team: finding, hiring, training, and managing all the different parts in the healthiest way possible. But we'll begin with the most important element—the horses.

## Horses with Issues Working with **People with Issues**

**H**orses are the element that brought me into equine assisted therapy. Our work rehabilitating and rescuing horses drove the search for finding a format in which their gifts could be utilized to the fullest. Through my work with rescue horses, who often cannot be ridden, I learned that relationship with horses on the ground could be just as remarkable—if not more so—than relationships in the saddle. The Parelli model reinforced this for me. I knew there had to be other people putting that same discovery to use.

The horses we have at *Horse Sense* are primarily rescue, rehabilitated, and adoption horse—that's how it all started. Our original goal was providing a good home and work for horses with difficult pasts. The rehabilitation process starts with each horse's physical situation before we address his emotional and mental issues. It's then we really find out what his personality is.

I personally think rescue horses have special gifts and abilities to offer in therapy. It rarely fails that a horse's past doesn't make him ideal for a client with a similar human past. For example, we have one horse in the barn who is our "boundary horse," consistently capable of measuring and testing the boundaries of our boundary-challenged clients. Rumor has it (and it's always rumor until I've met the horse!) that this horse had his boundaries violated by his previous owner.

For us, rescue horses shape the larger metaphor for our client philosophy: just because a horse can't be ridden, or a child doesn't make straight "A's" in school, doesn't imply that their gifts are useless to our society. Even the most "damaged" horse has the ability and the resilience to contribute, with proper care and attention. The same goes for the client.

As you really come to understand horse behavior and psychology, you may see your share of horses that have experienced abuse, mishandling, and poor treatment. Mental illness or dysfunction in horses manifests itself in displaced behavior not unlike the behavior you might see in a client. This brings out another important metaphor for me: that as an ES I can always better understand what might be an appropriate response for a client when I look through the lens of what I might do with the same problem in a horse. It becomes my touchstone. If a client were "stuck" mentally or emotionally in session, chances are they're also stuck physically. I would ask myself, "What would I do if this were a horse?" Well . . . I would ask the horse to move his feet, at which point I have my answer: I need to get the client to move their feet to get unstuck.

We consider it our responsibility to maintain the mental, emotional, and physical health of our horses. The dignity and integrity of the horse must remain intact if he is to be effective in a therapy setting. At *Horse Sense* we make sure each horse is sound in these three areas before putting him into play with clients. It's the ES' responsibility to monitor this.

## Training for the **EAP/EAL Horse**

I field a lot of questions about what kind of horse would be right for equine assisted therapy, and my answer is simple: in my opinion the only horse that *wouldn't* be right for this would be the "dead broke" horse. By this I'm referring to a horse whose natural instincts have been removed via some sort of training. I am reminded of a woman who was delighted and proud to demonstrate that her horse wouldn't respond when she deliberately tried to scare him. I am also reminded of the horse who refused to respond even when a live bear was presented to provoke a reaction. Aside from the fact that I darn well want my horse to respond when he's in danger, I feel strongly that it's inappropriate and unnatural to train the natural instincts out of a horse.

Again, a horse's natural instinct is the single most important element of the therapy session. It is crucial that their natural instincts are intact because it is *from* their natural instincts that we and the clients are drawing information. It gives us all clues as to where we should go. For instance, when we first started doing sessions, we would bring 3-5 horses into the arena and let the client choose the horse to work with. We never stopped to ask ourselves why we were bringing horses in from the pasture. Eventually we began experimenting with taking clients out to the pasture, out to the horses, and letting the sessions transpire in a more natural environment for the horse. We found that the simple change of allowing the horse to be in his natural place made sessions different than when only in the arena. When we change the horse —by changing his environment—we automatically create different dynamics. Although multiple clients in one day often necessitate bringing several horses in for a day, we always do at least some of a client's sessions out in pasture.

It sometimes surprises people that there is no other special training for therapy horses beyond making sure their temperament is safe for working around people. Unlike therapeutic riding horses, who need calm, quiet temperaments desensitized to wheelchairs, ramps, and unstable riders, training for EAP/EAL horses is more about un-training.

For example, so many horses today are trained to be robots, micromanaged to the point where they have no responsibility. They put their body in the appropriate position, then check out mentally while their body performs the necessary task. Some riders don't necessarily want to engage the emotional or mental aspects of their horse in accomplishing this task; they just want the physical performance. The more heavily trained a horse has been, the more time we spend inviting them to come back from "performing" and return to more natural behavior and instincts.

*Horse Sense* uses the Parelli system of horse psychology to unravel that. We seek to meet the whole horse, where he is. First we establish a safe environment physically. Then we begin the process of developing a relationship through the use of specific techniques like "undemanding time" and the Parelli "Friendly Game." Next we ask for permission, then watch for signs as the horse registers and processes this shift in communication. We are constantly reading the horse's body language as we work through mental engagement and curiosity to build confidence. In this way, our "un-training" of the horse progresses from being all about the "performance," or the human's agenda, to being all about the "relationship." This process is just the first step toward making a horse suitable for partnership in EAP or EAL.

The process is extremely powerful. Once you awaken true mental engagement in a horse, the next step is to be prepared for handling the subsequent reaction. Once we've given the horse the invitation to be in a true relationship, the initial response from the horse may be to develop stronger opinions, or challenge you in the same way they would challenge and interact with another horse in the herd environment. This behavior might come in the form of horse-like "dominance" games or other forms of behavior that would typically be met with disciplinary action in the world of ordinary horse/human interaction. Unfortunately, a horse's idea of play is often thought of as "inappropriate" by people's standards. However, we need to stop and recognize what's *really* happened: that the door has opened to something deeper than the "normal" horse/human relationship. We recognize it as the first sign of success . . . then move forward from there.

Obviously this process constitutes the early journey with the rehabilitated horse, and takes place far from actual EAP clients. At this stage of rehabilitation, it's all about the horse.

When a rescued horse arrives at *Horse Sense*, we don't begin working with him immediately. Usually there is a 'landing period' where we give the animal space to recover himself. He will most likely start out in our rehab barn, surrounded by other horses in the pasture while being safely separated in a stall. Our first priority will be physical recuperation, addressing injuries, weight issues, nutrition deficits, vet and farrier care. Then we stand back and let nature take its course, allowing the horse to regain his physical health while becoming acclimated to the rhythm of life at the farm. Depending on his situation, he might spend anywhere from several weeks to several months in physical rehab, before we really begin addressing anything else.

We realize a horse's true personality probably will not come out until the horse becomes physically well. The quiet, subdued horse you may have rescued might be a very different horse after he is physically sound. For that reason we begin directly addressing the mental and emotional side of rehabilitation only after the physical condition is normalized. Not surprisingly, therapists sometimes experience this with human clients as well. The client who comes in dysfunctional, traumatized, and quiet, may be a very different person once they get well.

Many of the horses we get remain in a disassociated state after regaining their physical health. Through abuse—and through the over-application of traditional

**UN-**DESPAIR

STATE OF NORTH CAROLINA
**DEPARTMENT OF JUVENILE JUSTICE & DELINQUENCY PREVENTION**
Buncombe County Courthouse Suite 801
Asheville, North Carolina 28801
State Courier No. 08-91-68
Telephone: (828)232-2564    Fax: (828)232-2562

Michael F. Easley
Governor

George Sweat
Secretary

Intervention/Prevention Division
Donn Hargrove
Assistant Secretary

Brenda R. Logan
Chief Court Counselor

November 8, 2005

To Whom It May Concern:

As Chief Court Counselor in Judicial District 28, I would like to encourage the funding of Horse Sense to provide services to clients who are on commitment status, Post Release, involved in Commitment Programming, or in risk of becoming committed to the Department of Juvenile Justice. My staff and I have developed a strong working relationship with the staff of Horse Sense and are very impressed with their non-traditional therapy options. For many of our clients, they have been in and out of treatment programs until they can manipulate the process by telling everyone what they believe they want to hear. This therapy option allows over institutionalized clients to be put in a very non-traditional setting and progress in treatment in ways they never thought they could. If we are to continue serving the most challenging juveniles of our state, we need to begin to look at alternative therapy options in order to help the most difficult clients move beyond the barrier they presently face.

In addition to their therapy options, Horse Sense offers some creative team building activities that may assist with getting clients to work together. These clients are sometimes handicapped by their lack of abilities to work as a team for a common good. The team building activities could help them to learn to appreciate the value of being a team player.

Should you have any questions about our experience with Horse Sense, please feel free to contact me at (828)232-2564. We sincerely appreciate your consideration in funding this creative way of treating our clients.

Sincerely,

*Brenda R. Logan*

Brenda R. Logan
Chief Court Counselor

*A letter written in support of Horse Sense for a local grant.*

training—they have been taught to carry out demands in a variety of circumstances, told what to do and how to look good doing it. They have learned, in effect, not to be present. The Parelli system works to bring back the disassociated horse because it speaks the horse's own language and to his innate nature, drawing out their curiosity and personality, asking the horse to truly engage. After we get through all the coping defenses the horse has developed, we finally arrive at the natural animal, the horse who is ready to give the gift of his natural self. That would be the special training we speak of . . . the *un*-training.

Once the physical rehab is established, we then begin work to prepare the horse mentally and emotionally for consideration in the program. My husband Richard is in charge of all aspects of each horse's rehab, although I'm involved as much as I can be, because I love watching horses "show up" and seeing all the different personalities. While managing our herd of fifteen horses, our hay and grain operation and management of our ninety-acre farm, Richard is also currently finishing his Parelli Level III, and hopes to attend the Parelli University program to work with difficult and challenging horses. His natural skill and ability, combined with a strong work ethic and a commitment to the whole horse, make him a wonderful and important component of our program (and a great partner).

Once the horse has gotten the "OK" at this point, then the *Horse Sense* team is given the green light to begin spending time with the horse, observing how the horse reacts and engages with people. We assess their 'horseanality,' looking at what they do when they get scared or confused, where their thresholds and hot buttons are, how easily they regain composure when presented with an uncertain or new situation. During this Horseanality session, each of us fills out forms adapted from a Parelli equine psychology workshop. We ask questions about the horse and fill out the forms individually, then get together and discuss why we answered the way we did and what we've seen about the horse from an EAP/EAL perspective. Through the process, everyone becomes more familiar with and more aware of the horse in question, possibly learning things they hadn't noticed before, or some additional information that might prove useful in client sessions.

## Do Horses Burn Out?

I get the question of "Horse Burnout" quite often. Obviously, if a horse becomes physically ill or unsound, they are and should be removed from duty immediately. But then there are some horses who start showing signs of needing a break without showing signs of any physical problem. An ES might notice a horse becoming or appearing a little dull or unengaged. If that happens, we'll rotate a horse out to the rehab barn, or take him out of circulation unless a client is extremely compelled to choose him. Sometimes the cues a horse gives us are incredibly subtle, so we always err on the side of caution. It's always a good idea to have enough horses in your herd so that pulling somebody out of circulation doesn't cripple the program.

We try to circumvent burnout and other such situations by making sure we balance our demands on the horses with a relationship-building exercise Parelli calls "unde-manding" time . . . perhaps the equivalent of "quality time" parents spend with chil-dren. For example, we can do this by taking them out of the pasture to a nice sweet spot of grass, sitting with them, and not asking for or directing anything on our part. We can take them for a walk, and let them decide where to go or when to stop. We can spend extensive time grooming the horse who loves it. The rewards of undemand-ing time are many, and profound, and go a long way toward building trust and relation-ship with individual horses.

Overall, I'm less concerned with exercising my horses physically than exercising my horses emotionally. The Parelli games provide that mental and emotional stimulation. Physically, I don't want them to languish, but neither do I need them in "competition" form. At *Horse Sense*, our steep hillsides, pasture environment, and herd dynamics work to give the horses plenty of physical exercise. We may work with a horse to overcome challenges with conformation or movement, and we do ride for pleasure those that can be ridden. However, exercising horses for the sake of exercise isn't at the top of my list. It's important that we're stimulating the horse in a variety of ways, and it's important we work on relationship and not just "work."

This is the part about equine assisted practice I remain most passionate about: horses that have use and purpose to offer the world without anyone ever getting on their backs. Far from mere "throwaways" or simple beasts of burden, the unrideable horse still has tremendous gifts to offer. There are those who have evolved theories or put esoteric labels onto this dynamic, but for myself, I know that when horses with issues connect to people with issues, remarkable things happen. I don't know how this happens; I don't necessarily *need* to know the how and why of it. I just know that it exists.

If you'd like to learn how to work with rehab and rescue horses, volunteer at your horse rescue. If you don't have a horse rescue in your area, you can go to the local Humane Society or animal shelter. Many of the principals for rehabbing dogs and cats will apply to rehabbing horses. The American Association of Equine Practitioners has an excellent article about equine rescue guidelines written from January of 2005. You can request a copy of the article by sending an email to the following address: aaepoffice@aaep.org. Request the article titled "AAEP Guidelines for Equine Rescue and Retirement Facilities."

## Hiring a Team: Practicalities First

**T**he remaining part of the EAP/EAL team is the human part: your employees. I once heard the saying that employees are your first customers. If they aren't happy, your clients ultimately won't be happy, or be able to create the kind of long-lasting change we hope for. Given the work we do, if anything is too far out of kilter within our team, positive change and lasting impact won't happen for the client. Eventually, it will come through in sessions. Employee happiness has direct correlation to client experience.

Creating happy employees starts by treating them like your first line of customers, and *that* begins with providing the basic practical necessities that allow employees to focus on their jobs. The first consideration: the debate of hiring full time vs. part time.

There are different philosophies that play tug-of-war with the new business owner in this situation. You can hire more people part time without providing benefits, or you can hire a smaller staff full-time. Obviously it's more expensive and complicated for a new business to have full time employees, but in my opinion there are numerous benefits that affect the quality of your program. If I hire full-time, I'm able to hire a more qualified staff, especially when it comes to hiring therapists. It would be easier to find and keep a talented therapist or ES if they're working full-time. Those people are here if I need to do an off-hours session; there's no conflict with another part time job. I feel a full time person will be more willing to go the extra mile, especially when the business is small and everyone has to do more.

Personally, I feel it's hard to demand someone's full attention when they're only working part time. I believe employees will be more committed if they feel a commitment from their employer in return. And, coming from my past as an adjunct college professor, I have a strong aversion to the way our system treats part time employees—an expense item to be over-used and overworked. So I work hard to hire *Horse Sense* employees on a full time basis. If I'm not providing what they need, and they've got to go elsewhere, then I'm not doing my job.

I believe in paying well and compensating fairly, trying to take the main worries out of my employees' world. However, knowing what I know now, I would probably be more careful about salaries, starting lower in order to have room to go up. My concept of money in the early days was tied to creating the best team possible no matter what the cost. I chose to go the full-time route; however we could have been more judicious.

One of the first things I did at *Horse Sense* was to get health benefits with Blue Cross/Blue Shield, including dental and some chiropractic, among other things. Offering health care is often a difficult undertaking for a small company, but it's worth the price, especially when you consider that losing an employee to injury or illness could hurt your company worse than providing adequate insurance coverage.

Workman's compensation is another practicality when it comes to employee health, and a legal requirement once you've reached a certain size. Each state has different laws, so make it your responsibility to follow the laws and rules. If you don't have the proper workman's compensation, you've really done a disservice to your employees *and* you'll be in a world of legal trouble. It's not negotiable; it has to be in place.

Continuing education is a huge priority for each *Horse Sense* team member, written into our staff policies, and easier to justify with a full-time staff. I happen to believe strongly in investing in the team; if we're not learning, we're stagnant. For that reason, there has always been a heavy emphasis on education. While that requires a substantial investment, it has been crucial to building our expertise and keeping the team satisfied and cohesive as a group for the long haul.

We attend trainings, workshops, and symposiums together. We've gone to Epona, to a McCormick's workshop, to EAGALA conferences, to Parelli clinics, and to trauma workshops. For each event we attend, our ability to function as a team improves. We talk, we brainstorm, we process, and we have fun. And together we bond as a staff. Continuing Education keeps employees engaged in their work at *Horse Sense*. It's worth the investment.

Our vacation package is quite good, and if I could create more paid vacation time, I'd do it. Due to the slowdown during the holidays, *Horse Sense* doesn't do much business during the end of the year so we take a week off at both Thanksgiving and Christmas. Employees also have two full weeks off between February and September. It may seem extremely generous, but it goes with my philosophy that we have to refill the well. If we don't take care of ourselves, we're not taking care of our clients either.

The other benefit of having a full time staff is that everyone is open to versatility and cross-utilization. In the beginning everybody on the team wore three or four hats, taking on duties that include program development, marketing, outreach efforts, presentations, and workshops, among others. There is still a fair amount of cross-utilization in our business today. They do it because they're dedicated to their profession and to *Horse Sense* as a business. We've worked hard to set up the best team possible, and tried hard to make them "our best customers." I think the philosophy is working.

## Non-Compete **Agreements**

***H**orse Sense* **has invested thousands of dollars in training its staff, something that's been both a choice and a necessity for meeting my goal to build one of the best teams in the industry.** One of the handicaps in this burgeoning field is the whole "learn-as-you-go" aspect, with amazing amounts of information developing at lightning speed from both the therapy and the horse side. It's exciting to be part of this and exciting to have so much new material to learn.

But it brings up a sensitive topic for your business as well. Equine assisted practice is such a new industry that nearly every person entering the field needs significant training to meet the standardization and certification being developed to give our industry credibility. Perhaps someday there will be a pool of people—trained, qualified, and certified—from which to hire. But until that point is reached, it may be up to organizations and businesses such as ours to make that training happen throughout our organizations.

How do you protect the dollars you've invested in training your team, getting them qualified and certified for this field? What can you do to prevent that investment from walking right out the door to compete with your organization?

Non-compete agreements are a bit like prenuptial agreements—not nice to think about, but standard in many other industries. There's nothing particularly revolutionary about utilizing them in your organization. If you invest money to significantly develop an employee's skills and knowledge in equine assisted practice, you deserve to find ways to get a return on that investment, or at least have that investment applied to advancing your business for a certain period of time.

The most appropriate time to utilize a non-compete agreement (or some other compatible form) is upon hiring a new employee. Have it be part of their opening paperwork, and use it to set a clear understanding up front about your expectations in regard to training and your investment in that employee. While it's my understanding that the enforcement of non-compete agreements varies by industry, it may be helpful to have something in writing with both your signatures to start things off on the right foot.

## Employee **SOP Manual**

**W**e've been both good and bad about our Standard Operations & Procedures (SOP) manual, but in general it's a really important document that everyone in the office should become familiar with. As your business grows, it becomes one of the important elements of continuity throughout your organization.

At *Horse Sense* our Employee Manual and SOP Manual are basically the same document, and it's taken various forms since the business opened. It currently contains a list of job descriptions, job titles, and expectations. We list employee policies like sick days, vacation time, weather-related situations, and reviews. The rest of the Manual has to do with specific procedures: scripts for taking phone calls, answers to common questions, client flow procedures from first call to exit interview, and tracking sheets. Basic, common sense stuff like this should be in one reliable place.

## Meeting **Schedules**

**A** big part of managing our team comes in the form of structured meetings. Once your organization grows beyond two people, it becomes important to create forums for regular communication.

Initially, we held several kinds of meetings: clinical meetings for therapists and specific case studies, ES meetings, and horse play sessions. The play sessions were fairly important when we first opened, as they afforded greater opportunity to get to know the horses who would become so integral to the team. As equine specialists, we needed to see how each horse responded to stimuli, how tolerant, playful and/or sensitive they were. We had to be able to recognize subtle differences in behaviors that would provide clues during client sessions, and warn us of individual horse issues before they became serious.

Horse play sessions became formalized after a certain point, and were used as sessions for trying out new activities and exercises, using the horses and each other as models. We would work on developing skills as ES's and therapists, similar to role play in EAGALA training. It was good to see things other people were picking up and noticing, and conducting open dialogue to fine tune our skills.

We also held weekly "core" meetings, an emotional check-in period designed to put everyone in touch with their emotional states and bring the staff closer together. While the concept was good, the emotional check-in period started to become unwieldy and even uncomfortable over time. Sometimes we simply learned too much about each other, and what was initially a good idea intended to help us be more "congruent" actually started to put too much focus on ourselves.

Our core meetings today are less touchy-feely and more professional, with an agenda that incorporates aspects from the full "menu" of meetings for scheduling, clinical reviews, case studies, and horse play sessions.

## The Ins and Outs of **Working with Friends**

**I**f an employee isn't a friend when they come to work at *Horse Sense*, they **usually become friends at some point** through the sharing of mutual passion and interest in our work. But this dynamic presents some challenges as well. A common feature of many equine assisted businesses in development is that they are started by friends who become business partners; there are even a few husband and wife teams, which present another set of circumstances.

If you're going to work with or hire friends, know that there's potential to lose that friend somewhere along the line. My experience has been that having clear boundaries with the work relationship and the off-work relationship is really important. For the best interest of the clients, a working relationship needs to be a professional relationship first, with a personal relationship that is kept clearly separate. But that's not your biggest challenge: the greatest danger in working with friends is the problems you can't foresee or even imagine in the beginning. Your philosophy about horses might be the same, but your work ethic might be totally different. Your personal work styles may clash, or your approaches to conflict resolution may be incompatible. Discovering these differences can be an ugly process that's devastating to the program, putting everyone from horses to staff to clients at odds. And the resulting hurt—because it *is* personal in nature—can have personal and professional repercussions you can't imagine.

One of the best ways to approach a friendship-turned-business relationship is to begin with the end in mind . . . literally the end, in this instance. I know of people who have sat down at the beginning of their professional relationship and talked about everything that could go wrong with the partnership. They've planned, in great detail, what they agree to do in each instance—how they will handle problems and resolve conflicts. They even plan how they will "break up" if necessary, and split both hard assets and intellectual property. One lawyer puts it very nicely: decide *how* you will break up while you're still friends. Of particular interest may be the book *Fierce Conversations* by Susan Scott.

All of this said, given the choice between hard and strict boundaries or occasionally needing to restate and redraw boundaries with employees/friends, I'll take the latter. If I'm going to err on one side, it's going to be too close, not too far. That's my personal preference; yours may be quite the opposite!

## Finding **the Right People**

**S**o where do you look to find qualified people?** *Horse Sense* has found success in several areas. The local school systems are one place to find strong therapists, people especially adept at thinking on their feet and handling a variety of situations. Therapists from social service agencies and clinics have become interested in EAP or EAL after participating in one of our Continuing Education Unit sessions or demonstration days.

The therapy world is full of people suffering bureaucratic burnout, ready to leave an overloaded case schedule and apply their talents to an intriguing form of therapy in a less-confining situation. Finding a pool of candidates is less difficult than making sure they are the *right* candidate for your program.

Finding an ES is generally not as hard as finding therapists. However finding *good* Equine Specialists can be as hard as finding good therapists. I have found potential ES candidates by participating in events in the local horse community, attending training opportunities, and Parelli events. If I'm looking for someone specifically interested in EAP, I'll look for them at an EAGALA event. In regard to *Horse Sense*, ES candidates usually find me, not the other way around.

# The Long **Interview Process**

**I**n a small organization like ours, it's one thing to find qualified people, and another thing to make sure they're going to be a good fit.** We've had our share of mistakes in this arena, and it has taken some time for *Horse Sense* to develop a truly successful hiring process. One of the most effective tools we use now is a long interview period, one that eventually involves the whole staff, horses included.

Our interview process starts out with the normal face-to-face interview following a résumé screening process. If that goes well, we invite the interviewee to participate in a team play day. An EAP team facilitates the play day group session in which the whole team, ideally, is present to interact with the interviewee. We can begin seeing how the person works, what their patterns and compatibilities are, and envision how he or she might fit within the team.

I ask the interviewee to give me written feedback after the session: what they observed, felt, or thought about. I give them no rules, leaving it wide open to see what they choose to bring up. The feedback really gives me a feel for the person as the more formal barriers of the interview process start to come down. I can get a good glimpse inside the person's thought processes and reactions. I can also begin to notice any red flags. If a significant issue comes up at this stage, we end the process.

The next step is to schedule an individual session for the candidate with one of the horses and a therapy team. The session is followed again by written feedback from the interview candidate and the staff, giving us their feedback on how the session went. Of course the candidate will react differently in an individual session vs. the first group activity. This session gives us the opportunity to learn different things.

The single most effective aspect is to put the new candidate with the horses, and then let the horses tell me what we need to know. Just as they do in a regular client session, the horses reveal a person's true patterns beyond paper credentials or references. These sessions tell us everything else we need to know about a candidate's sense of feel, timing, sensitivity, empathy, and all of those intangibles critical to success on our team. Any undiscovered red flags pop up during these sessions, revealed quickly and effectively by the horses themselves.

While we're looking for our perfect candidate, we also know this is an extremely intense process for the interviewee; we recognize that it will be stressful and try to be respectful and sensitive to the situation. In all of this, it's not a matter of right or wrong behavior on the part of the candidate; it's about "can I live with what I see?" Is the person more concerned with the relationship with the horse than with being effective? If so, can I live with that dynamic? Are they more concerned with not making the horse mad than with taking care of their safety? Are they valuing what I'd like to see valued in our business? Again, it's all information.

Hiring is completed with a 30, 60, and 90-day review process that ensures our decision is a sound one for both the employee and the business. The review process gives us the opportunity to open dialogue, make assessments, and course-correct.

## Maintaining the **Mental and Emotional Fitness** of Staff

**S**o here you have the big picture: we go to great lengths at *Horse Sense* to hire the right people for our staff.** We work hard to give them adequate salary, benefits, and support. We provide ongoing training and professional development for their continuing education and engagement. Now it's my job to maintain that.

I look for people who know how to have some sort of a balance in their life. Given the nature of our work, I know how vital it is that we practice what we preach, that we work to keep ourselves mentally and emotionally fit. We once hired someone who worked with us two days a week, and had another job for four days a week. This meant she had one day a week off. I knew the situation was not viable long-term, so I kept track of it. I knew that ultimately it wouldn't promote a healthy lifestyle for her, or give me the kind of person who could continue giving their best. She eventually cut back to one day a week, giving herself two full days off, which I heartily supported.

Equine assisted practice is not supposed to be about us . . . and yet if we're not totally balanced, healthy, and present, we have the ability to mess things up pretty easily. This isn't to say that employees aren't allowed to fall apart from time to time; everyone has trying situations in their lives. We just try to remain aware of our individual situations, to ask for help, to practice good self-care. And we try to stagger challenging things in our lives so they don't all happen at the same time!

I'm looking for lots of intangibles in the employee's ability to maintain self-care. Are they able to say "no?" Are they able to state what they need? Do they practice healthy eating, healthy exercise, healthy balance of work and play? A person who doesn't do these things isn't going to last long in my program, and they may not be long in the business because it's not in the best interest of the client. I pay attention to these aspects of my staff. After all, we're in the business of mental health. And the mental health industry has plenty of examples of those who neglect their own issues in order to serve their client's ultimate best interests. But in sacrificing themselves, they don't serve their clients . . . or they don't serve their clients *for long*.

An unhealthy or unbalanced team might not ruin your business right away, but it will certainly make things ten times harder and make everyone miserable beforehand. That, for me, is the number one reason why you want to have a good, healthy team.

## Fostering **a Good Team**

**I**n equine assisted practice, we are by nature a team. We don't work by our-selves. Even if you're practicing EAP by yourself, it's always you and the horse. I've talked about how *Horse Sense* has used continuing education as a team building tool. Traveling to and from seminars, meetings, and conferences as a team is a bonding experience in itself. Airline flights, car trips, shared meals, even shared hotel rooms put us face to face for extended periods of time. Sharing new information or insights brings us into alignment and puts us on the same page.

Like Parelli, I strive for extreme "middle-of-the-roadism," a center between "touchy feely" and "cool and professional" in the office. We stopped using emotional check-in sessions for staff which, over time, became an inadvertent form of deep group therapy sessions that went beyond simple team building. However, creating an "emotional check in" tool might be appropriate for your organization, especially in your early development. It's a good way for your team to get to know each other. Just be aware that beyond a certain point it may become counterproductive.

A resource I've enjoyed on the subject of fostering a good team is Patrick M. Lencioni's book, *The Five Dysfunctions of a Team*. It provides some food for deep thought in examining both obvious and not-so-obvious factors within your team, within your business, and what you're putting out there for clients. It also provides some refreshing discussion on trust, team buy-in, and giving everybody a choice and a say.

I would recommend having a standard procedure for conflict resolution, both within the general staff and between the Therapist/ES treatment team. Part of our process at *Horse Sense* is to hold a debriefing at the end of each client session, which gives the team a chance to check in, verify, and go over things that could have been different while discussing what should be accomplished the next time. Good communication between the therapist and ES is pretty important, and we have found that a debriefing session helps to clear up misunderstandings and clarify things before time erases the details. With a scheduled debriefing session, you can reduce the need for formal conflict resolution a great deal.

AA's core concepts of "HOW" and "Principles Before Personalities" are effective for nearly every situation we encounter. "HOW" stands for Honesty, Open-mindedness, and Willingness. When the team needs to iron out an issue, we automatically apply these three aspects to our resolution process. "Principles Before Personalities" reminds us to focus on the issue rather than ourselves. Doing what's right is more important than our individual egos.

Being part of a team is kind of like being in a marriage: you're going to disagree on some occasions, perhaps strongly, and being able to have a tough, engaged, impassioned discussion without going into crisis mode is important. Our first protocol revolved around the 3-part filter: "Is it true? Is it kind? Is it necessary?" If I can answer "yes" to all three of those things, I can probably go ahead and say it. And my teammate on the other end can trust me to follow the protocol, which makes *both* of us more receptive to hearing the other. If a comment doesn't meet these three criteria, it's probably being said for reasons that are inappropriate. So that is one very effective filter we use. If you run a comment through the filter, and can't affirm that it's True, Kind, and Necessary, you can then run it by a supervisor for verification.

Receiving continuous feedback, support, and supervision is a crucial part of what we do. And although the practice of mentoring and apprenticeship is fairly standard in the therapist world, I strongly support EAGALA's new procedure that requires all practitioners wishing to go beyond a basic EAGALA introduction, both equine specialists and therapists, to receive mentoring supervision specific to Equine Assisted Psychotherapy. Just like your SOP/employee training manual, having adequate mentorship helps establish baseline knowledge and provides a level of continuity for the staff. I also happen to think it's a good standard for equine assisted practice as a field.

For the lone practitioner, finding appropriate feedback, support, and mentoring supervision can be a real challenge, although the resources *do* exist. Just like any endeavor, finding a support network of similar practicing EAP/EAL counterparts is something you have to cultivate with real intention. Ask for mentoring. Participate in every learning opportunity. And find ways to obtain honest evaluation on a regular basis.

Here's a few of the other *Horse Sense* Guiding Principles that steer our actions as a team:

✳ **When in doubt ask the horse.** Whenever you're not sure what to do, ask the horse, and use his reaction as your guide. After all, isn't that why the horse is such an ideal therapy tool? The horse reflects clear reality back to us. They don't play games. They aren't prey to our illusions. When lack of clarity is clouding your mind, find a way to put the issue to the horse, and the answer will become apparent.

✳ **How we treat the horse is how we should treat the client, and vice versa.** This goes beyond the obvious question of what is considered ethical and proper in our treatment of both horse and client. This paradigm always helps us when we are "stuck" in process. If I don't know what to do with the client, I'll stop and ask myself what I would do in this same situation if it were a horse. And vice versa. We aren't speaking of anthropomorphism here. We are speaking of a core principle based on the assumption that the horse and client are mirrors for each other. In our experience, reframing an issue in this manner often helps reveal its solution.

✳ **If it's about us, we're doing it wrong.** In EAP work, our sessions always, *always* need to be about the horse and the client. Professional detachment on the part of the therapist and the ES is crucial. If focus in a session starts to become about us as the therapist or the ES, something has gone off track. By becoming too much a part of what's happening, we made a wrong turn somewhere and have ventured out of bounds. I have seen this happen when either the therapist or ES are burned out or struggling with issues that cannot be contained outside the session. This should be a red-flag signal to the team that something is amiss. If the therapist or ES carry baggage into the session, the horse will reveal the discord, and the session will be robbed of effectiveness.

✳ **If it's about us, we're doing it wrong, Part II.** This dynamic can also become a danger when people use their own horse, or even project their *attachment* to a particular horse, in therapy sessions. Detachment is a hard thing to do for people who love their horses. In a therapy session, you turn your horse over to someone else. You allow their interpretation to inform what is happening. Respect the fact that this may be hard to do; *know* when it begins to interfere. If you cannot detach yourself from either the horse or from your own issues for the purpose of this therapy, it becomes an unethical and undermining element that compromises the program's respect for the client, the horse, the therapist, and everyone else. Again, the horse will reveal the discord in short order.

## The World of **the Therapist**

*In order to give you the clearest picture from a therapist's point of view, the comments in this section come from* Horse Sense*'s own lead therapist, Rob Jacoby.*

**P**erhaps the greatest difference between traditional models of psychotherapy and EAP is the shift from conducting therapy as an individual to therapy as a team. Although some forms of traditional therapy include co-facilitation, the co-facilitator is also a trained therapist. In the EAGALA model, the Equine Specialist often has little or no training in human psychology nor the psychotherapeutic paradigm. In addition to co-facilitation, there is now the third and most important element: the horse or horse herd. The shift has moved from one-on-one therapy to at least a three-member treatment team plus one or several clients. EAP parallels group therapy work in that the clinician must be prepared and flexible enough for anything that transpires in the group. The therapist must incorporate everything that the group offers into a therapeutic moment.

Moving from traditional therapy practice models to EAP requires a great deal of patience, flexibility, and faith from the therapist . . . faith that the model works. EAP utilizes open-ended questions by both the ES and therapist directed at the client to understand what is transpiring between them and the horse in that moment. The patterns that surface during the EAP sessions mirror the same patterns created by the client in their lives, which leads to perhaps the other great shift from traditional models. Instead of delving into an individual's history concerning trauma, unresolved pain, success, and failure, the EAP model stays in the moment. How an individual conducts himself or herself in the present moment during an EAP session with the horse is how they live their lives. These are the patterns which are identified by the EAP treatment team.

Traditional therapy relies on many factors to be even mildly successful. First, the therapist must build rapport with the client, eliciting enough trust and respect so that the client feels safe enough to disclose pertinent and sensitive information. Depending on the client, the issues, and the therapist, to list only a few of the possible confounding variables, this could be a long and drawn out process. Once core issues and detrimental patterns of behavior are believed to have been identified, the process of therapy can begin through learning new and functional patterns.

The second major challenge in traditional therapy is eliciting disclosure and reliable self-report from the client: self-report on the core issues that cause the destructive patterns of behavior. The third challenge is trusting that the client is actually incorporating and practicing the newly-learned patterns into their lives, and accurately reporting their progress. Most of this process is privy only to the client. The therapist oftentimes has limited means of verifying what the client is doing between sessions.

Looking at the EAGALA model, everything changes, such as strong rapport with the therapist, accurate and reliable self-report, and most importantly the practice of new healthy patterns of behavior. The relationship between the therapist and client is no longer the key element in successful therapy. With the EAGALA model the relationship that the client has with the horse is the primary focus. It is now not about the relationship with the therapist. One of the biggest benefits this offers is it takes away the strain and pressure of establishing effective rapport with the client and, by stepping out of the mix and formula, the therapist facilitates learning through the relationship that the client has with the horse.

The EAP model instantly removes the necessity of reliable self-report. The therapist can instead observe the client by paying close attention to what the client's behavior reveals during the session. This eliminates any question the therapist has regarding habitual patterns of behavior. We see it. Within a single session, the client and treatment team identify patterns of behavior, process information about the pattern, and immediately begin practicing a new pattern with the coaching of the treatment team present. Traditional models have not offered this dynamic. The three major challenges of traditional therapy have been overcome.

There are a few areas where the co-facilitation team aspect of EAP impacts the therapeutic model. First and foremost, there are now two sets of eyes to watch what is transpiring between the client and the horse. This is crucial since the model is experiential and one individual cannot observe everything that is transpiring. Secondly, there is no question on the client's part as to what patterns they are creating, as there are now two individuals and a horse offering immediate feedback.

Next is the issue of rapport. Where traditional models rely heavily on rapport-building and establishing trust between the therapist and client, EAP is focused on identifying and changing patterns, thus creating growth faster than traditional models. In a nutshell, the session moves faster and with accelerated results. Through focusing on a client's relationship with the horse, the client can modify patterns, oftentimes in just one session. In traditional therapy, this process could take anywhere from weeks to years, depending on the rapport between client and therapist.

When executed with fidelity to the model for EAP, it is the client that feels that they have come up with all the answers, not the therapist, and in doing so gives those answers a weight and credibility they wouldn't have coming from outside of themselves. When a client is able to identify patterns and provide the solution themselves, the changes are far more poignant and long-lasting than if a therapist delivered those same solutions sitting across a desk, saying, "I know what your problems are and here are the solutions and what you need to do to practice them." Again, *Horse Sense* teams live the metaphor of becoming the "table setters" in the client session. Once the client shows up for their session, we simply take a step back and do what we can to facilitate the session without being the major focus of the session.

It is amazing to see how the same horses can react in totally different ways from one client to another. We try to rotate horses throughout the day, but on those occasions where we use the same horses for back-to-back clients, it only provides further affirmation that the insights gained from the horses' feedback are not a fluke. If the horses acted the same from client to client, we would be compelled to question the limitations of those insights.

Again, through a process of asking open-ended questions of the client, we see the horse very clearly mirroring the next client's issues in a completely different manner. And we see them do it accurately, successfully, and very clearly time and time again, in ways that defy scientific basis or explanation. Somehow horses have a capacity to be so open, so completely in the present moment, and so completely without attachment, that they can reflect completely different realities from one client to the next, even with only a short amount of time between clients.

## How **Equine Assisted Models** Relate to the Therapist

**E**ssentially, what makes a good therapist in equine assisted practice is an individual who is flexible, a team player, passionate about the art of psychotherapy, and above all dedicated to relearning almost everything they ever believed about psychotherapy. The right therapist must willingly accept the challenge of looking at their own issues, patterns, and faults like never before. Finding the right therapist becomes crucial, as this is where most of the work begins in creating a dynamic and effective team.

There has always been an understanding that to provide good therapy, the therapist needs to embark on their own therapeutic journey of self-discovery and self-awareness, taking a look at their own judgments, preconceived ideas, and core belief systems. Part of that learning process is examining the principles of projection, transference, and counter transference.

However, as much as a therapist might feel they understand these concepts, it often isn't until they start practicing the EAGALA model that they realize how much of a part they play with clients. The EAP modality, specifically, commands that the therapist be constantly assessing their own issues, constantly re-evaluating who they are and asking questions of themselves, "How much of this is me? What am I projecting? Where is the transference? Where is the counter-transference?" It is crucial for the team to pay attention to projection, transference, and counter-transference because the horse as biofeedback is not only assisting the client in evaluating their own patterns of behavior, but echoing as a secondary sounding board for the therapist in ways they might be interfering with the client's progress.

With the EAGALA model it is necessary for the therapist to be mentally, emotionally, physically, and spiritually healthy, centered and balanced. This is yet another striking difference between the equine assisted practice model and traditional modalities. Not only is the client able to be in a non-judgmental, safe, supportive environment to explore their own patterns, but therapists are also being challenged to do the same. The growth and experiences of the client in these sessions parallel our own need to examine needs for power, control, projection, transference, and counter-transference, etc. After years of therapy experience, the typical therapist may or may not realize they are drifting into exhibiting, acting on, or struggling with these same things. In equine assisted practice, the horse insists that the therapist is clean.

It is the EAP team's job to make sure the delivery of therapeutic services is effective and long lasting so that it will hopefully facilitate a more fulfilled life for the client, based not on our definition of fulfillment, but the client's.

Again, it is crucial that both the therapist and the ES be healthy, emotionally, psychologically, and physically to accomplish effective EAP and EAL. If the two are not in a healthy, functioning, and professional relationship, the dynamic will become very clear, very fast to both the horse and the client. The horse will react to the individual who is the most incongruent. EAP is not the ideal model for the therapist with the "wounded healer" pattern. In fact, this is the last place that a therapist rooted in the belief that effective therapy comes from control should be. Equine assisted practice requires humility, and doing yourself that which your clients are asked to do. Continue to work on who you are, and how you live your life.

Being a healthy team is only the beginning. The next aspect of the healthy EAP team is how they communicate. Once the team has a strong foundation in terms of individual health, including healthy boundaries, then they can work on increasing the flow of their internal communication. It is almost as if the treatment team takes on character roles which accentuate and highlight the EAP session, and this can only be done with healthy team members who are committed to mastering this unique art of treatment.

Probably one of the more important aspects when searching for a therapist is finding an individual who has some post-Master's experience as well as footholds in the mental health community. Having some recognition and credibility in the mental health community definitely helps with securing funding and referral sources, especially if one happens to live in a rural area where innovative and non-traditional therapies are not commonplace. It is good to find someone with post-grad experience practicing and understanding traditional psychotherapeutic models. Although both therapist and ES undergo an "un-training" from traditional modalities, it is still important that there is education and experience in the core foundational concepts of psychology and psychotherapy. It is important to know what a front door is before teaching someone how to use the side door.

## The *Horse Sense* **Therapist Job Description**

**T**herapists at *Horse Sense* **conduct client assessment and evaluations.** Psychological assessments take place in the office using traditional psychosocial tools for gathering a client's pertinent history. From there the therapist creates a treatment plan based on the presenting issues. The client directs this treatment plan, as the client sees it, which is then revised and honed by the therapist and client together.

In developing the treatment plan and goals, we look to the presenting issues that the client brings to treatment, and then create tangible, attainable goals, which will be accomplished throughout the treatment process. Goals, or new skill sets, fall into categories of communication, conflict resolution, coping skills, emotional awareness and management, problem solving, assertiveness, self-esteem, and empowerment. Typically we allow eight sessions after this assessment to address core problems before evaluating again. If the client is a public referral, we adhere to the agreed-upon structure the client is being seen under.

The therapist matches the appropriate ES to each client after first knowing what type of client the ES is comfortable working with. Once this is done, it is just as important to match the client with an ES that will be conducive to effective sessions. This develops into an effortless process as the therapist becomes familiar with the various members of the ES team. The therapist should become proficient at gauging what populations are best for what ES.

## **Trading out** Therapy Service

**O**ne aspect of equine assisted practice that presents itself is the offer to **trade out therapy for other services.** As a rule, this should be avoided altogether. EAP is a powerful form of psychotherapy. Issues arise, and even in EAL sessions these can quickly border on the edge of therapy. In short, if an individual wants to experience EAL or EAP via a trade arrangement, it is best to offer a tour or demonstration, or refer them for further education. The dual-relationship ethical concerns that are (hopefully) indoctrinated in all professional therapists applies to equine assisted practice just as it does in traditional settings. Therapists should not trade out for psychotherapy. Avoid and avert dual relationships at all costs. If ever there is a question about the nature of a relationship, seek supervision.

(Rob Jacoby has been with *Horse Sense* since September of 2005.)

# The **Equine Specialist**

**The Equine Specialist in equine assisted practice is one who utilizes their education and knowledge of horse psychology and behavior** to observe the horse's reaction during a client session, and reflect their observations to the therapist or to the client in the form of open-ended questions. They do this by reading situations from the horse's point of view without anthropomorphizing (projecting human feelings unto the horse.) The ES strives to be a student to the horse, continually studying with and learning from horses over a lifetime.

According to the EAGALA definition, an ES differs significantly from traditional horse professionals such as instructors and trainers. Traditional horse professionals teach people to model themselves after another person or an ideal rather than to be themselves: "Be like me, learn how to do it like me." Some traditional horse professionals train and work with horses; others work with people to improve skills, whether in riding or some sort of technical proficiency with horses, showing the student how to be more effective in whatever it is they are trying to do. The ES, however, does not teach horsemanship skills, a fact that is hard for many horse people to grasp. The job of the ES is to help facilitate an equine assisted process whereby the client learns healthy life skills. Their job is to exist in a world that has less to do with a "right way" or "wrong way" than about removing interference, so that the horse can be studied for reaction and feedback to a given client situation. It is not about the task, but about the process.

## **Attributes and Trouble Spots** for the ES

**Like the therapists, there are a number of desirable attributes and potential problem areas that can crop up for Equine Specialists.** From a purely practical sense, the most ideal background for any ES is someone who's been a hands-on caretaker of horses themselves: someone who's had to wake up at five in the morning to feed on a cold winter's day before going to work, someone who's had to be there when a horse colics in the middle of the night, or has had to wait when the vet is three hours late. The process of just living with horses and taking care of a small herd, day in and day out, for several years, is terrific training. In contrast, spending a handful of hours in the saddle while someone else boards the horse is not going to provide nearly the same understanding of horse behavior and psychology as being their primary caretaker every day. Least desirable is the person with a lot of technical proficiency in dressage, eventing, reining, cutting, or competition without any behavioral horse psychology or skills from the ground. There is little chance this person will have the complete, well-rounded understanding of the horse that I'm looking for.

I look for how an ES candidate cares for their own animals: how they take the needs of their own horses into consideration, if their horses are kept in an open pasture environment or are stalled, and whether they are kept solitary without companionship or in a herd. I look at these things as a reflection on that candidate's deeper beliefs and considerations.

I also look for a person whose mind is open to the possibility that certain things don't always have specific and rigid meanings. I stay alert to certain catch-phrases and responses that indicate a very traditional mindset based on old assumptions, phrases like, "you have to show them who's boss," "don't let them put one over on you," or "you can't let the horse win." Likewise, I look for any evidence of training with the horse that involves force, intimidation, or mechanical means that push the horse into performing or holding himself in a certain way. If someone believes these methods are appropriate or necessary to work with a horse, they probably aren't a good fit for our approach.

However, the main qualities of a good ES are less tangible and harder to pin down with specifics. The most important asset of an Equine Specialist is the ability to read both horse and human body language during a client session and then apply that knowledge to provide feedback as necessary. The practice of EAP is all about the team-work between ES and therapist in reading both human and horse body language from moment to moment, based on their individual expertise in both human and horse psychologies.

Overall, the professional Equine Specialist should be a student of horses, horse behavior, and horse psychology. We look for the person whose personal stance toward horses is that of a "lifelong apprenticeship," dedicated first to the horse's well-being, and second to the agenda for the day. I look for horsemanship as it relates to the welfare of the horse, not in riding skills. A good ES has a basic humility that allows him or her to be open to learning more. In fact, an ES does not have to follow a particular discipline or a type of riding; skill in the saddle or show ring isn't necessary and doesn't guarantee anything. It may, in fact, be a detriment if the person has been overly-indoctrinated into traditional beliefs and patterns that might limit their openness to the interpretation of horse behavior.

A savvy approach and intelligence with the horse on the ground is critical for an ES. This person has to display an understanding of why horses respond the way they do, and further acknowledge that each horse has a completely unique personality with distinctly unique boundaries and limits. We can learn a lot simply by observing the way someone catches and halters a horse and leads him. Can they tell if the horse is confident or unconfident? Do they know when to approach and when to retreat? Do they know how to utilize their own body language to communicate with the horse? If they have these basic skills, chances are they have the basics to recognize when a horse goes into fight-or-flight mode, and how to diffuse a potentially explosive situation.

A problem area in ES candidates is anthropomorphism, the temptation to project human characteristics onto an animal that is very different from us. Horses are not people; they have different processes and paradigms. Dog specialist Cesar Millan has a great discussion of this topic in his book *Cesar's Way*. I would recommend reading it to gain a good understanding of what this is, and how it impacts the Equine Specialist's ability to be effective with horses.

It's also important that an ES respect the horse's ability to take care of him or herself without human intervention. Underestimating the horse in this regard ranks right up there with anthropomorphizing, and displays an elemental disrespect and misunderstanding of the horse. I don't think that the horse has any trouble taking care of himself, nor does he need to look to me before making a move. My job is to make sure the horse has the opportunity to take care of himself, including always giving him a way out of the situation. In EAP, the best thing that we have going for us is the horse's natural instincts. If I have to insert myself to get my horse to respond, then we have defeated the whole process.

The flip side of this is the treatment of the horse as a means to an end. This is something not uncommon in traditional training barns and trail ride strings, where it's not about getting the horse sound or safe to serve the horse's best interest, but about using the horse to serve the business' best interest. If the horse is treated as a means to an end, we are objectifying the horse. I believe the horse is a partner in this process and not a beast of burden, an inanimate object like the ropes in a ropes course.

One way to screen for this trait (or an overall dominant mindset toward horses in general) during your interview process is to ask the following question: "What has your horse taught you lately?" or "What is the most recent lesson that your horse has taught you?" If that question doesn't register an immediate response or a thoughtful pause with your ES candidate, I would take it as a precautionary note and begin looking for someone else. If a candidate doesn't listen to his or her horse, they are probably not going to listen to a partner, a therapist, or clients. There is no reason to suggest that things will suddenly be different when they are in an actual client session.

A closed-minded, "know-it-all" attitude toward either horses or humans should be a red flag, especially anyone showing outright antagonism toward any belief or system. You might see in this in the debate of "western" vs. "English" riding, or "Parelli" vs. "John Lyons" . . . as if this were politics instead of horses. Having strong opinions is one thing; being totally closed down to ideas outside one's paradigm is simply another definition of ego-based intolerance.

Both ego inflation and codependency are especially dangerous for the Equine Specialist . . . and dangerous for our industry as a whole. It can be hard to suppress the desire to display knowledge and understanding when the client, in awe of the situation, looks to us for answers. However, inserting our beliefs, our knowledge, and our structure for the purpose of massaging our ego is not appropriate; it's what the client interprets in this situation that's important. Being all-knowing, smug, or self-satisfied doesn't serve the client. It closes the door and locks things down for them. Many of us, myself included, have done this at one point or another. The important thing is to recognize it as it happens. We need to monitor ourselves, for as the 12-step philosophy says, "You spot it, you got it."

This is especially challenging for those who have a strong "codependent but clueless" syndrome. These are well-intentioned people who can't resist rushing over to help a client when they're struggling to put a halter on the horse, who need to *make* the client be successful. We're here to facilitate and support the client succeeding on her own. Acting out in order to get our needs met—in this case "helping" the client be successful—has no place in equine assisted practice. The therapy industry has enough trouble with people who operate to feed their own dysfunctions. It's more important to "teach a man to fish" than to give him a fish that only helps for one day. This does not mean, however, that we never assist in the process, if appropriate.

It is troublesome to see an ES candidate who is trying to play therapist. The ES is not a therapist; that's not their job. There are many levels to this problem in our field. Granted, we all know there are enormous benefits from being around horses, and a great potential for personal development. But when an untrained person assumes they have the wherewithal to get psychologically messy with a client, it is ethically wrong, period. Having knowledge around horses does not make one proficient in dabbling with potentially serious issues in the lives of other people. I strongly encourage anyone thinking about working on their own using EAP or EAL as a personal development tool for other people to get really, really clear about the profound differences between coaching, personal development, and therapy. A clear delineation of those boundaries is crucial.

Even within a healthy ES-therapist team there is an important balance to maintain. If the horse specialist regularly tries to take over client sessions, something is definitely amiss, indicating transference and counter-transference issues that need addressing. The ES provides insight in partnership with the therapist, but the therapist needs to guide the session.

## The Marriage of Natural Horsemanship and Equine Assisted Practices

As I've mentioned before, I became a big fan of Natural Horsemanship a long time ago, and use the Parelli methods due to their emphasis on horse psychology and the fact that their organization is the first to put Natural Horsemanship into a curriculum that can be consistently and effectively taught to other people.

Our goal in equine assisted practice is to utilize the horse's greatest gift, its natural instincts, to provide us with biofeedback in working through client issues (among other gifts). The goal of most Natural Horsemanship is to work with the integrity of the horse's being in its most natural state. These two disciplines meet in a very effortless way that works compatibly toward both goals.

Once people get on the back of a horse, the horse's choice to respond in a natural way becomes automatically limited. Communication shuts down to whatever point the rider ceases to listen, providing they are listening at all. Subtlety is lost. The accuracy of the horse's biofeedback is compromised.

It goes back to the basic philosophical reasons of why equine assisted practice is so effective from the ground in the first place: skill in the saddle does not necessarily translate to ability on the ground. By being on the ground, we're on a level playing field with the horse. For that reason, familiarity with the basics of Natural Horsemanship is a key component for anyone I consider as an Equine Specialist. Many fluent in Natural Horsemanship prize ground skills over saddle skills, and promote the study and understanding of the animal first and foremost. They come to EAP and EAL with a built-in humility that recognizes learning from horses is a lifelong study . . . not something to be conquered overnight.

Again, I recommend *The Revolution of Horsemanship* by Dr. Robert Miller as one of the best resources available for those becoming familiar with the basics of Natural Horsemanship. I also recommend Dr. Miller's *Understanding the Ancient Secrets of the Horse's Mind* to understand more from the horse's point of view.

## Recommended **Reading**

*5 Dysfunctions of a Team*, Patrick Lencioni

*Cesar's Way*, Cesar Millan

*Fierce Conversations*, Susan Scott

*Understanding the Ancient Secrets of the Horse's Mind*, Dr. Robert Miller

## Building **Awareness:** MY **STORY** continued

**I** *call it the "M" word. Marketing, that is. When we first started out, I started with two big chips on my shoulder when I thought of marketing.* The first is that I didn't think I had to do any marketing. I thought the cream would rise to the top, and that if I built something really good, business would just materialize out of thin air. The second misconception that I brought with me was the thought marketing was "unclean," something that was too commercial, carried out by sharks in suits, not something little do-good organizations like ours did. I thought it was about playing tricks on your audience, capitalizing on people's fears, and appealing to a base mentality.

I had to get past the concept that marketing was bad. Even worse, I had to face the reality that in order to get people to the barn I needed to get out of the barn. I had to go places and participate in events and meet with groups of people, not something I relished.

Once again, our "just do it" mentality went to work. We used the phone book to find all the mental health professionals, counselors, therapists, addiction centers, and clients we thought we might want to serve. Then we mass-mailed a survey to them. We wrote a brochure and put print ads in several different publications, most of them freebie magazines and newspapers you get at the local bookstore. We listed free tours and demonstrations in community calendars, and invited both the locals and health professionals out. I called the local magazines and TV stations, inviting them out for what I hoped would be news stories and some publicity.

My idea was to generate name and logo recognition, to build awareness of who we were. It turned out that some of the things I did by instinct were right on target. But some of the things really missed their mark, too. Until recently, our print ads, for example, weren't at all effective in telling people what we did. People saw a name, and they saw a photo, but the ads didn't do the job I paid them to do. We even had a few minor disasters. The Yellow Pages ad, for example, misspelled the word "experiential." From the outset I questioned whether or not I should use the word "experiential" in the ad or not. Then I went back and forth with the proofing

101

*department correcting the word, because they kept changing it to "experimental" instead. I thought we finally had it fixed... then the ad came out and there it was: the words "experimental therapy" big and bold as you please. And the complete opposite of the message I wanted to send. To make matters worse, it happened two years in a row! We got a free year of ads because of the mistake, but I can only image what people thought: "Come in, let us experiment on your daughter!"*

## Getting Past **the "M" Word**

**T**he truth is you will probably—eventually—get business if you do no **marketing at all.** But it will come slowly, and you probably won't survive the wait. And while the *thought* that being a Good Samaritan program means rising above the need for marketing was all wholesome and good, I eventually had to face the fact that *nobody would find us if they didn't know we were here.* It was as simple as that.

So I had to get over it. And just like everything else, I learned how to do marketing by making a lot of mistakes and spending a lot of money. However, I also did quite a few good things, and overcame many misconceptions in the process. I'm hoping this chapter might help steer you through those same pitfalls and down the right roads, in the right order.

Most businesses start out by getting a logo, business cards, and maybe getting a website. That's exactly what *Horse Sense* did, but what I *should* have done instead was take the time to develop a strategic marketing plan and spend more time trying to accurately discern what potential clients really wanted. That would have put me in a better position before I began spending money. Websites, brochures, and yellow page ads are fairly important in the early stages of your business, but only after you've decided *how* to use them.

In addition, I learned about a philosophy for marketing that's a bit different from the traditional approach: the concept of *drawing* customers to your business vs. *driving* them to your doorstep based on the book *Attracting Perfect Customers* by Stacy Hall & Jan Brogniez. The aspect of attraction vs. force made marketing much more appealing to me in this sense.

When you're brand new, you can usually design your own logo, register your domain name, build a very simple one- or two-page website, and put your name in the phone book. It doesn't have to be very sophisticated. But now I know that when you put a little more thought into it, you can get *so much further* with the same effort and money.

This year, *Horse Sense* has utilized the more formal services of a writer/marketing consultant—a member of our Virtual Team—to develop a marketing plan for the business. We underwent a strategic planning process that helped us clearly define our needs with razor-sharp focus, then developed those needs into goals and an action plan. The process took about three months and substantially improved effectiveness, helping us reach our target clients with less effort and less money than our "shotgun" approach ever could.

Realizing that many newer organizations might not be able to afford a full-blown strategic process, I had our writer/consultant (who is also the co-writer of this book) create a simplified process that can be utilized by equine assisted practices and programs just getting started. She broke the marketing process down into six basic steps that even the smallest organization can execute with some measure of confidence. What follows is her simplified process, ideal for the fledging organization. Here's the steps we'll be outlining:

**Step One:** Plan

**Step Two:** Develop the Message

**Step Three:** Develop the Materials

**Step Four:** Implement

**Step Five:** Track

**Step Six:** Repeat

## Everything You Do Is Marketing

**What is marketing? It's anything and everything that tells people about you.** Ideally, marketing is supposed to provide information, show how you provide a service, and attract customers to your business.

So the first thing you need to realize is that pretty much *every activity you undertake is marketing* in one form or another. In other words, everything you do communicates who you are: the way you answer the phone, your program's t-shirts (that you might wear to the grocery store), the presentation of your facility, and the way you talk to people about your business. Marketing is communication, both tangible and intangible. And when you think of marketing, you need to consider how effectively *all* of these things are working, either for or against what you want to project.

It starts with yourself, and how you act in the world as a personal representative of your business. Marketing then begins to take other forms as you strive to communicate your message beyond your personal space. This would include the ad you put in the paper or the yellow pages, the radio commercial, the story done by the local TV station news. It's your logo, your business card, your brochures, your billboard, and the press release when you win an award. It's also the grant proposal, the power point presentation, and the sign at your front gate.

All these things have power . . . the power to communicate your message, build your presence, and enhance people's perception, or power to erode.

## Step One: "Just Doing It" vs. "Doing It Right"

### Think things out first, don't just "do it."

**W**hen people skip this step of their marketing, you can bet they'll be wasting their money and not even realize it. Just like writing a Business Plan, when it comes to creating their marketing efforts, most people will be tempted to ignore any sort of planning process. And who can blame them? Just like business plans, marketing plans have been mystified and complicated to the point of being overwhelming.

So you put the ad in the paper or write your brochure, not realizing that the most important customer might not even read the paper you've chosen, or get the message you wrote. You might miss your mark entirely. You've spent money you can ill afford to waste, and received no return on your investment.

### Find Out What the Market Wants

**W**here you want to serve and where *can* you serve may not be the same thing. The first part of any marketing process is to find out what the market wants . . . and finding out if it even matches with the services you provide. This may take several weeks, or even a couple months, from start to finish.

Of all the things I did in the early days, sending out that first survey was one of the best (a copy of that first survey is included in the paperwork online). You need to know what the community wants and needs. You need to get their most basic thoughts. Without this key piece, your marketing efforts from start to finish could be completely wrong. Develop a questionnaire that outlines the basic information you need to collect. Send it out using Survey Monkey or other websites. Then compile your results. Some of the survey websites compile this data for you, which is tremendously effective (since that's what they specialize in.)

Hopefully you've got an idea both of where you want to serve and where you think you can serve, because this will impact the survey you send out. You may even want to send out several surveys in different areas focusing on different populations. Maybe you have one survey focusing on parents for their kids, or another that taps into mental health for adults.

Another way to test your potential populations is to conduct focus groups. How do you conduct a focus group?

✳ If you want to work with adult women, you can do something as simple as getting a few of your girlfriends together.

✳ You can use processes and questionnaires gleaned from marketing books that specialize in this area, or you can actually hire a marketing consultant.

✳ Or you could target a more specific group and go through a more formal process.

The important thing is to find out what your client populations would want from you, and how they react to the program you are suggesting.

The third way to find out what the market wants is to go out and conduct one-on-one visits to your target markets. Talk to different therapists, corporate groups, and organizations. Ask what their level of interest would be for your program. Have lunch with them, or find a way to attend a group conference and talk to people in individual conversations. This method, however, entails talking to a large quantity of people. Don't make assumptions from just one or two people; be sure you get opinions from a well-rounded audience.

**Set up a Mailing List**

**O**f course, your whole marketing process starts with determining the population of possible clients you want to do business with. This, in turn, will determine who you will market to. This process entails doing the basic groundwork of tracking down and finding all your mental health care providers, therapists, schools, agencies, or other broad populations necessary for your business. You're going to need to know who these people are, so you might as well plan on spending a couple weeks digging up the information. Use the phone book, use the Internet, use a database/ mailing list expert, or go to the library. Create a mailing list of all the organizations, individuals, and agencies that will use your business. Pick up the phone and find out who the pertinent contact people are, and get their email addresses. Then keep adding from there.

**Utilize the "Thinking" Process, not the "Guessing" Process**

**I**t's important to undertake some sort of strategic thought process to figure out the simple aspects to your marketing. Start by listing the follow basic things:

1. What are the needs of your community? How do you know they even want or need what you plan to offer? Use the results of your survey process to write out your findings.

2. Who are you? What does your organization do? How many different kinds of services?

3. Who is your customer?

4. How many different types of customers do you have? Is there a different customer or group of customers for every service you provide? List them.

5. Who else is competing for those same customers? Is it another equine program on the other side of the county, or is the outdoor adventure therapy business down the road?

6. How does the competition advertise? What tactics do they use? What can you do to make yourself distinctive from them?

7. What are the implications of each item above? What does it mean to your business?

## Make a Grid

**Take another piece of paper and create a simple matrix that breaks your customers down into their different segments.** Write them across the top of the page. For *Horse Sense*, some of our customers are doctors, therapists, mental health facilities, and juvenile institutions. Yours might be churches, families, and women's groups. Now examine each group a little more closely. Under each group, list the following items:

1. What are this group's needs?

2. What are their issues?

3. Who makes the buying decision?

4. What is the best way to approach that customer?

5. What motivates them to come to you? How do we appeal to them?

6. What is the biggest obstacle that prevents them from using your business?

7. How do we reach them? Do they read a newspaper, use the Internet, or watch TV? Which TV station would they watch? Which radio station would they listen to? Which newspaper would they read?

8. When is the best time to talk to them? In the summer? During the school year?

9. How do you talk to them? Do you use a specific language? Do you use a specific type of voice? Is that voice formal, professional, or casual? Do you use humor? Comfort? Hard facts and figures?

Professionals call this process strategic planning; I now call it common sense. And it represents the huge difference between fly-by-the-seat-of-your-pants marketing and strategically-correct marketing. If you don't plan, you are marketing by guesswork, assumption, and chance. If you DO plan, you're using rational thought to make very specific decisions. You're making sure that the money you spend is put in the right places, where people will actually *find* you and be most receptive to hearing your message.

This strategic process needs to take place every year, at least 3-4 months before your new fiscal year begins. The information from this process should be used to update both your Business Plan and your Marketing Plan for the coming year.

A business plan is the document you put together that contains the broad brush strokes of what you see the business doing. It's the "big picture" of everything you want to accomplish, with the nuts and bolts items that include financial projections, and program offerings. In contrast, the strategic plan is a more precise document that changes year to year, based on the challenges you're facing at any given time. It has timelines and task lists for implementation. The strategic plan outlines key issues and a series of tactics, strategies, and tools to address those issues. It gives you a tremendous amount of focus. It allows you to be clear and precise about what you're doing.

From a marketing standpoint, a strategic plan gives you a clear focus of who you're going to talk to, how you're going to communicate to them, and what goals you're trying to accomplish, in crystal clear language. It helps you avoid what we started out with, which was trying to be all things to all people. Be clear about who you are and what you do, and then focus on communicating what is important.

Many businesses are tempted to use a "shotgun" method in their marketing and advertising, thinking that it would be better to hit everyone than to sow seeds in specific places. *Horse Sense* did this in the beginning, and while it helped create overall awareness, it took a long time to build the most basic retention among the general public. Even then, they didn't understand what we were. We were spending our money to try to reach everyone. We had no money left over to really be effective.

It's a far better strategy to *know* who you need to reach, learn what motivates them, and develop a specific message that appeals to that segment of the market. Every dollar you spend on advertising and marketing will then be targeted and leveraged to its highest potential. You don't need to reach everybody, nor should you try. You need to reach a "productive" audience . . . one that has the highest probability of responding and bringing business to your doorstep.

As your business grows and matures, your strategic planning needs to mature with it. You may eventually want to utilize someone who's a professional in strategic planning and marketing . . . someone who can help you make more thorough and sophisticated decisions on producing collateral, buying media, and generating publicity.

## Step Two: Develop the Message

**Message: Information that creates a shared understanding about what you offer**

**Marketing: Activities that get your message to the right audience**

**S**o now you know who your market segments are. You've defined each segment, evaluated what appeals to them, and what aspects about your business will draw them to you. Now you need to formulate that into a message that puts everything into focus with cohesive statements.

In other words, you need to develop the message . . . and you need to do this *before* you try to market, before you try to print a brochure or build a website, before you speak to the local organization, before you get interviewed for the story on the local news. Skip this step, and you'll end up wasting valuable opportunities speaking to your market using a voice that doesn't fit their style, using language they can't connect to, or missing a key point. Your message will lose its effectiveness. It won't be heard. You can't market if you can't communicate!!!

For example: You know that you want to attract business from doctors. You know doctors will be interested in hard facts, proven results, and return on investment. You know you will have to speak in professional terms, and that emotion will have little value. So you build your message using these parameters.

Or maybe you're appealing to families, and you know that they will be interested in hearing about both the practical and emotional benefits of using your program and how it will affect their child. You will use a more informal approach in your language and tone. You might interject more emotion, or tell a story.

The three people who started at *Horse Sense* each had their own area of specialization. Two of us were really strong in work with addictions, one of us was strong in work with at-risk youth, and one of us strong in work with adult women. So what did we try to do? We tried capturing all three in one big ad rather than realizing that each market segment needed a slightly different approach.

### Features vs. Advantages vs. Benefits

**O**ne mistake people make when they talk about the message is that they focus on the "how" and not "what" of their business. Talking about how you do EAP is like talking about a part on your car without ever explaining what benefit that part gives the car's passenger. Which brings us into the discussion of Features, Advantages, and Benefits.

Understandably, how we do what we do is extremely interesting to people. However, what we do is also difficult to translate for the uninitiated. And when we get so excited talking about the "how" and forget to mention the reason why this should be even remotely interesting to other people, it becomes even more challenging to understand.

One *Feature* of EAP is that it uses horses in an experiential setting. One *Advantage* of EAP is clear, immediate, unbiased feedback from horses. Another *Advantage* includes EAP's effectiveness with unresponsive, treatment-resistant, or treatment-savvy clients. Or perhaps that EAP works within a shorter time span, making it more cost-effective for clients. But the *Benefits* include overcoming anxiety and fear, learning to be fully present in our bodies, and developing effective coping strategies to conquer problems.

In discussing what we do, it's fine to talk about *Features* and *Advantages*. But to be really effective in motivating our client, we need to talk about *Benefits*, and we need to talk about them *first*. The *Benefits* talk about how EAP and EAL impact our clients and improve their lives. That's what they really care about.

## Step Three: Develop the Materials

**G**o back to the matrix you developed above, and use the information to decide what kind of materials you need for your marketing. What is the most effective way for them to get your message? What kind of media do your target clients use? Is it a radio spot for soccer moms who spend the whole day in their SUV driving? Is it a one-on-one presentation piece of networking with professional groups? Do you need to reach kids? Business professionals? Therapists and doctors?

Go back up to Step One and re-read: everything you do communicates who you are. Everything you do has power . . . the power to communicate your message or to destroy your message.

If you invest money anywhere, invest it in good marketing materials. A good graphic designer is an essential part of your Virtual Team, as are good website designers, good photographers, and a good writer. If you're thinking of doing video, find a video production company. In every case, no matter what form of marketing collateral you seek to develop, find multiple freelance people. Interview them, get multiple prices. Ask to see samples of their work. You should see a wide range of talent—or lack thereof—and pricing when you interview, which is why it's essential to interview 2-3 people per discipline. Find the best fit for price and style, then *let the professionals do their job*. The complications and pitfalls of producing video, audio, websites, logos, and brochures are far too complex to go it alone.

However, do not allow these professionals to start creating marketing materials until they've had a chance to review your strategic paperwork. Walk them through your discoveries; they need to have a thorough understanding of *who* your audience is and *what* your message is. They will need this information, along with a good understanding of your organization, to effectively design, shoot video, or write for you.

Keep in mind that your materials don't have to be the most expensive or have the most bells and whistles. You can keep things basic and simple. Just make sure they are well done.

## Step Four: Implementing Your Marketing

**O**nce your message is clear and your marketing materials are produced, there are multiple ways of implementing efforts to get your marketing going. Let's break it down into "passive" marketing and "active" marketing.

Radio commercials, newspaper ads, TV spots, newsletters, and publicity are forms of *Passive Marketing*, otherwise known as Advertising. You buy space and place the message in a customer's environment, and make yourself available to them. You hope that your message attracts them or compels them to take action of some sort. To build a baseline "level of awareness," you follow certain formulas to build frequency and repetition to make sure the customer is exposed to this message on a consistent basis. You then make your website and phone number available so that customer can get more information if they desire. There are two forms of Passive Marketing: Paid Placement and Unpaid Placement.

When it comes to *Paid Placement*, the best piece of advice I can give is to use your strategic process to decide where, when, and how to do it. Don't buy a newspaper ad if your market segment doesn't read that newspaper! A common mistake for small business owners is to assume that their customer has identical tastes in music or programming. They then wonder why their radio or TV ad hasn't worked. Follow the ratings research, not your gut instinct.

*Unpaid Placement* is called Publicity or Public Relations, whereby you work to obtain favorable media coverage that helps spread the news about your organization. Local media continually seeks interesting news stories about their community. Businesses can find and utilize these opportunities any time they have something interesting or significant happen to their program: when you hire new people, host a tour, attend a conference, receive an award, or reach a significant anniversary or milestone. If you analyze your annual calendar, you can actually plan ways to use public relations throughout the year. Publicity is considered more credible in the eyes of the public . . . so much more credible, in fact, that it's value is one and a half times more valuable than the same amount of space or time bought through paid advertising. Get enough publicity, and your organization can supplement its advertising budget substantially.

## Active Marketing

**A**ctive marketing consists of personally attending events, meeting people, **shaking hands,** and telling people who you are and what you do in a concentrated period of time. This includes networking through business and community organizations and events, making presentations or speeches to targeted groups, or conducting onsite tours, demonstrations, and seed sessions.

This leads us to the second most feared word: Networking. Again, as I struggled with marketing I struggled with networking. My understanding of networking was the stereotypical "booze and schmooze" types of things. Networking was intimidating to me, or at least not the first on my list of things to do, which I suspect might be true for a lot of people. But I was finally able to understand a different perspective on networking, one that wasn't about struggling to find integrity and remain clear on who you are.

Still, few words strike as much dread in the hearts of an entrepreneur than networking. The prospect of facing a room full of strangers, trying to remember the advice of dozens of networking articles from business magazines, and the risk of making a complete fool of yourself is daunting. If marketing was a difficult concept for me to understand, networking was even worse.

However, Life and Business Coach Elizabeth Barbour sees networking a different way: "What I always try to remind folks is that networking is about building relationships. If you can focus on building relationships one person at a time, it can make a huge impact on the bottom line of your business." When you stop focusing on achieving an objective, and instead focus on connecting to the person in front of you, it begins the process of starting a relationship. It focuses on the possible long-term value of that relationship by learning about the other person before staking claim on a project or client. According to *The 7 Habits of Highly Effective People* by author Stephen Covey, "Seek first to understand, then to be understood. "

There are several different types of groups you can seek for your networking purposes:

✳ Professional colleague groups like EAGALA.

✳ "Wide Net" groups like your local Chamber of Commerce designed to help you get to know people from all areas of business.

✳ Focused Networking groups like BNI (bni.com) and Toastmaster.

✳ Service clubs like Rotary, Kiwanis, and Lions Club. Service Clubs help you develop deeper relationships with a small group of people that you meet on a regular basis.

✳ Volunteering and/or serving on Boards of Directors. The key to serving on a board is to do something that you love. It does not necessarily have to relate to your business. If you are an animal lover, volunteer at the Humane Society. If you love working with the elderly, volunteer at a nursing home. It does not necessarily have to be related to your business. However, keep in mind that one of the biggest things we do when volunteering for organizations is over-commit our time and burn out. That is why I emphasize choosing a volunteer activity that really brings you joy.

The value of being a member of different kinds of groups is you can establish relationships at multiple levels within your community . . . any one of which could become a valuable resource or ally to your organization. The most successful business people are those who network on a continual basis, establish good relationships in the community, and are able to reach key people within the community because of it.

Keep in mind that these same organizations are always looking for speakers and really interesting presentations. They might be the perfect opportunity to present your organization to a large audience. Luckily, the work we do in EAL and EAP is inherently interesting. It's fairly easy to talk about, easy to engage people. I'm not always crazy about everyone who shows up and the ways they network themselves, but I`m really comfortable with the basic philosophy and the design of how it works.

### Onsite Marketing

**O**nsite **marketing through live tours, demonstrations, and even some pro bono work** with key organizations are key to equine assisted businesses. No other form of marketing is as effective in getting people to understand who we are and what we do. Nothing translates the experience more effectively. Getting targeted client markets and key decision makers out to the farm is the single best thing that can happen. We'll discuss the various options and their pros and pitfalls in the next chapter.

## Step Five: Track

**S**o now you're up and running. It's time to track your results. At some point, you need to make sure you're on target, or decide how to course-correct. It's important to be able to measure response, especially over a period of time. And keep in mind that tracking doesn't just have to be for marketing purposes; it can help you make business decisions as well.

Set up a tracking system from the get-go. At *Horse Sense* we track things like number of phone calls per day and the most common questions and comments we get from callers. This simple tracking mechanism helped us make a key decision awhile back. We were open Wednesday through Saturday at one point. However, the number

## UN-DESPAIR

Two of our high-risk youths have already benefited from Horse Sense's therapeutic services, particularly in their demonstration of a significant reduction in number of assaults, fights, self-injurious episodes and suicide attempts. Moreover, we have seen major improvements in their interpersonal skills over the course of their 22 sessions at Horse Sense. One young man        , whose conduct included very frequent verbal and physical aggression toward others, gradually became a very positive role model and exhibited leadership qualities among his peers. The other        , who ha usually communicated to staff by a minimum of talk, often mumbling speech, and who had twice attempted suicide and made numerous suicidal gestures since arriving at our Center, now seems to have gained an inner confidence in that he ofte takes initiative to openly converse with staff, make appropriate requests, and refrains from self-injurious behaviors. We believe that the psychotherapy and interpersonal skills training received at Horse Sense has had a profound effect on these two students, and contributed to a deep healing of some childhood wounds that is now fostering their emotional resilience.

*A letter written to the assistant district attorney from the local juvenile detention center as part of our grant process for the Gang Violence Prevention Program we offer.*

of calls we received on Mondays and Tuesdays prompted us to change our schedule so that we now have someone in the office answering phones on Monday, and have added Tuesdays to our work week. In the same vein, keep track of the advertising you run, and see if you can find correlations between *when* people call (is it right after an ad runs?), and what *kinds* of questions they ask. Are they reading from the ad? Ask people how they find you. Are the ads attracting them? If they aren't finding you from the ads, and if they're confused after reading the ads . . . then you need to *change* your ads, and now!

Using website tracking is another common tool. There are a number of measurements that can be implemented for tracking capability when you build your site: how many viewers you're getting, where your viewers are most commonly going, and the length of time they spend on each page. And here's an idea: use your other marketing collateral to help drive customers to your website so they can get more in-depth information. Create a "call to action" in your print ads and brochures that invites people to check out the site. Say you run a newspaper ad about your upcoming Open House. See if you get spikes in your website traffic after running the advertisement.

If you're going to be doing advertising of any sort, ask people how they've heard about you. If everyone's finding out about you through one certain newspaper or publication over another, maybe you quit advertising in the other publication. Track what *kind* of people you're reaching. Is it mothers? Doctors? Teachers? Is your ad in the right place, or is it attracting the wrong audience?

We track demographics (age groups, male to female ratios, broad income levels, ratio of nurses to doctors, etc) of our audience during demonstrations. We also track the demographics of our clients who come for therapy (age, sex, type of therapy, etc.) We track payment methods (Medicaid vs. private pay vs. insurance). We track the number of clients per week. You could track number of sessions per client and evaluation results across an entire client population. Statistics like these come in very handy when applying for grants, or presenting your program to people who value hard-core statistics, like therapists, institutions, and doctors.

I also advocate more serious tracking mechanisms on a regular—perhaps annual—basis. Use Survey Monkey or something similar to check in with existing and past clients, medical professionals, or the general public. Find out if their perceptions and attitudes toward your business have changed significantly over the past year. Do they understand you better? Has your message been clearer? Do you need to make a shift in your marketing? Or maybe see if their needs are changing. Are they starting to ask for new or different services? If there's a new product you want to offer, send out a survey to see if people are interested before you invest in it.

## Step Six: Repeat

Like the words "strategic planning," the word "branding" has been complicated and mystified beyond necessity. Branding, pure and simple, is about consistency and building a solid perception of your business.

Put every piece of your marketing collateral on a table: T-shirts, brochures, printouts of your website, business cards, letterhead, printouts of your Power Point presentations, newspaper ads, radio spots, and your phone message script. Does it look like it came from one place? Does it *sound* like it came from the same place? Do the photographs have a consistent look? Do you use the same font? Do you use the same colors? Does each message use one set of key message points, the same tag line? Now extend it further: does each member of your staff answer the phone in the same way? Do they know how to talk to the public using a standard message and your key selling points? Does your message on the answering machine use the same announcer and music as your radio spots?

If you can say yes, congratulations! You've done branding. If, on the other hand, your material looks like it represents two or three different companies, you have a branding problem. Maybe you have a different person creating your newspaper ad every month, or maybe the radio station uses a different announcer and different music for each spot. Either way, you're failing the branding test.

What branding really means to your business is that you are effectively using your money to build a consistent identity with the public. So market well, market often, and—most importantly—market with simple consistency so that every investment works for you.

## Recommended **Reading**

*Attracting Perfect Customers*, Stacy Hall & Jan Brogniez

*Equinomics: the Secret to Making Money with Your Horse Business*, Lanier Cordell

*Guerrilla Marketing: Secrets for Making Big Profit from Your Small Business*, Jay Conrad Levinson

*Money, Meaning & Beyond*, Andrea Lee

*Small Business Marketing for Dummies*, Barbara Findlay Schenck

www.elizabethbarbour.com

## Building **Clientele:** MY **STORY** continued

**W**e used a shotgun approach when Horse Sense first opened its doors, which is a short way of saying we tried to be everything to everybody. From our very first ad, it's clear we were casting a wide net. Our very first calls reflected that reality. Five out of ten called to ask, "Your ad looks interesting, but who are you? What do you do?" Another percentage were people looking for a riding program. And still others wondered if we were doing energy work or animal communication with horses.

I've come to find out that even with the best advertising it's difficult to explain what equine assisted practice is through ads alone. The advertising needs to be in the right spot the right number of times. The language needs to be carefully thought out. And, you can't get caught up in telling people how you work instead of letting them know the benefits equine assisted practice can provide. You need all of this combined to break through the crust to the juicy pie below.

But we also realized we needed more. We needed to find ways to build clientele that included hands-on education of key people . . . people who were our most likely clients and the health professionals who would refer them to us. We needed to supplement our advertising by getting them out to the farm.

Our first real clients came to us through existing relationships I already had in place in the community. A girlfriend of mine worked with a local 4H group, and she referred four clients to us. We gave each client several sessions free of charge, which gave us a chance to work on our methodology and build client contact hours. One of those clients eventually turned into a paying client.

A personal relationship with a local criminal justice organization yielded work with a program called "Women at Risk," dealing with women involved in some way with the criminal justice system. The Women at Risk program brought ten women out to Horse Sense every quarter for a full day of activities. Our therapist partnered with the program's therapist to blend the EAP aspects into their therapy. It was a good combination of programs, and another big client for Horse Sense.

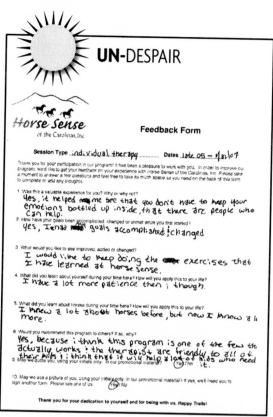

**UN-DESPAIR**

*Horse Sense*
of the Carolinas, Inc.

**Feedback Form**

Session Type _individual therapy_____ Dates _late 05 – May 07_

Thank you for your participation in our program! It has been a pleasure to work with you. In order to improve our program, we'd like to get your feedback on your experience with Horse Sense of the Carolinas, Inc. Please take a moment to answer a few questions and feel free to take as much space as you need on the back of this form to complete or add any thoughts.

1. Was this a valuable experience for you? Why or why not?
*Yes, it helped me see that you don't have to keep your emotions bottled up inside, that there are people who can help.*

2. How have your goals been accomplished, changed or unmet since you first started?
*Yes, I had goals accomplished & changed*

3. What would you like to see improved, added or changed?
*I would like to keep doing the exercises that I have learned at horse sense.*

4. What did you learn about yourself during your time here? How will you apply this to your life?
*I have a lot more patience then i though.*

5. What did you learn about horses during your time here? How will you apply this to your life?
*I knew a lot about horses before, but now I know a lot more.*

6. Would you recommend this program to others? If so, why?
*Yes, because i think this program is one of the few th actually works & the therapist are friendly to all ok & their kids i; think that it will help a lot of kids who need it.*

8. May we quote you, using your initials only, in our promotional materials? Yes No

10. May we use a picture of you, using your initials only, in our promotional materials? If yes, we'll need you to sign another form. Please see one of us. Yes No

Thank you for your dedication to yourself and for being with us. Happy Trails!

*A 15 year old soccer star who was in state custody and was struggling with grief and loss issues for her biological family. She has since been moved from state custody to a loving home.*

As I've said earlier, the biggest mental road block for me was the "M-word" of Marketing. It took me quite some time to get comfortable with the concept of marketing for my business, and I know it's true for many others as well. But it helps now to have a better understanding that marketing, at its core, is nothing more than letting people know your business exists through a strategic thought process.

The hair still stands up on the back of my neck when I refer to potential clients as "markets," but eventually I came to terms with the fact that I was in business to help those in need, and that I couldn't continue to serve them if *Horse Sense* ceased to exist. To reconcile this in myself, I reviewed the core philosophies informing *Horse Sense*. AA talks about "attraction rather than promotion." Parelli talks about causing the horse to catch you, rather than going out and catching your horse. EAGALA talks about learning occurring outside your comfort zone (and marketing and networking are *certainly* outside my comfort zone). As I looked at these philosophies, I found a theory of "marketing" that would work for me. Just as in working with horses themselves, I feel there's more integrity if clients come by natural attraction instead of through some sort of coercion . . . allowing people who need our services to find out about us. So now for me, marketing is all about carefully thinking through the ways a perfect client would best find us.

It's easy now to recommend having your marketing plan and a strong message in place prior to doing what *Horse Sense* did. The lack of clarity in our model showed in our advertising when we started out! I did the mass mailing to every therapist in the phone book. I had the fiasco with the Yellow Pages ad that misspelled "experiential" two years in a row. And I spent two years running general print ads in various publications. I advertised in magazines I read and wanted to be associated with. We advertised in the local animal magazine, the local women's publication, and the freebies that are available in lots of towns. We publicized tours and events in their calendars.

I learned that the likelihood of getting advertising messed up is high, and the likelihood of actually being understood is low. People thought we had great advertising, but it was only because they saw us over and over again. If you asked them more probing questions about us, they were lost. The resulting phone calls proved that our advertising, the way we were doing it, did not help people understand us, nor did it draw clients with any significant effectiveness . . . not enough to prove its worth. Something in the mix was wrong.

I know now that advertising has to go hand-in-hand with some sort of planning and thought. It also needs tracking to measure its effectiveness. Running the same ad over and over doesn't mean anything unless you know you're reaching the right people and giving them the information they need. When we started asking clients and callers how they knew about us and what they actually knew about us, we found a lot of misunderstanding.

Chapter Six was about the nuts and bolts of your entire marketing function. In this chapter we'll extend that to talk more specifically about certain aspects of marketing for EAP/EAL: ways to better define your potential clients, developing programs in specialized areas, conducting hands-on tours and demonstrations, and the marketing considerations for grant writing.

## Determining **Your "Market"**

**T**he most basic starting point for this is figuring out *who* you want to serve. Barbara Scott talks about learning about your community's demographics in her EAP business plan: the lay of the land, the numbers of the market, who you're hoping to attract to your program. I wish I had done a better job scanning the potential base in this way.

I knew I wanted to work with at-risk youth, and I also knew that a large group of potential clients was made up of adult women. I did the right thing by using my initial fact-finding and survey to determine if there was a need to fit the population I wanted to help. It goes without saying that if you want to work with aliens from Mars, you need to determine if aliens from Mars even exist in your area. You can't simply assume the population is there.

Even more importantly, do not assume you completely understand their wants and needs. Believe it or not, even large corporations have made this mistake, creating entire campaigns based on assumptions they thought were correct, only to have their customers correct them the hard way—by not buying—after the fact. All because they didn't stop to ask.

Go back to the fact-finding process outlined in Chapter Six to make sure you don't make the same mistake. Research your region, put out surveys, *talk* to your markets. If you're not sure about the information you get back, ask some more. Then use the grid from your strategic planning process to really think through the basic characteristics of each market. Once you know these parameters, they can keep you from making simple mistakes, i.e.: if you know that key decision makers for your market fit one demographic, why would you put an ad for that market in a publication they don't read?

The next section outlines a few of the broad potential clients available to equine assisted programs. As you read through them, start thinking about how each of these markets needs to be approached. Who are the key decision makers? What kind of language do they use? What kind of appeal would they respond to? Hopefully you'll begin to understand how important it is to tailor these elements to each group if you're to be heard, understood, and utilized by these client groups.

## Strategic **Places to Find Clients**

✳ Women form one significant client group for both EAP and EAL, and women's organizations are a good place to start. If you're serving this group, everyone from women's mentoring and business organizations to women's treatment centers to groups dedicated to specific women's issues become logical targets for your efforts. You may find that many of these organizations have programs, scholarships, or grants to help pay for services. Or they might hold a significant number of self-pay clients.

✳ Youth populations are another large and rewarding client group for equine assisted programs, although it's really a broad term for many different kinds of specialized programs. Youth-center programs can consist of at-risk and/or juvenile justice prevention work, learning disabilities programs, or programs to develop self-esteem and confidence. Many schools have classes for Behavioral and Emotionally Disabled (BED). Kids with a lot of learning disabilities end up in these classes and are great candidates for both EAP and EAL work because equine assisted practice addresses kids in a different way from traditional academic classrooms.

✳ Boarding schools or therapeutic boarding schools are a key market for EAP and EAL. Both types may already have a barn and horses as part of their program, but they may not be utilizing the horses in this way. Many of these schools easily recognize the value of adding EAP or EAL to their programs, and further recognize its appeal as a unique form of counseling and programming to parents.

Working successfully with schools means presenting your program to key decision makers inside the school before you ever get the opportunity to sell your program to the parents. For Equine Assisted Psychotherapy, school counselors are your first line of approach. For Equine Assisted Learning, teachers should be in your sights. Various school administrators and/or boards may have to enter the mix before a decision is made. *Horse Sense* did this by networking through our existing community contacts to find out who the counselors and teachers were. We then made direct contact to begin discussions. *Horse Sense* did pro bono work with the first school who utilized our services. Another school is paying for us with school funds. Various grants and scholarships are another source of funding for these situations.

✳ *Horse Sense* has developed both youth and adult programs with local treatment centers for addiction, recovery, and illnesses like eating disorders. EAP is also extremely appealing as a form of outpatient adjunct therapy for clients, being utilized for therapy clients "stuck" or spinning their wheels in traditional office therapy situations. Your program can offer a series of sessions for these clients in collaboration with a primary therapist to help move things forward. Adjunct therapy arrangements can be ideal for therapy organizations and individual therapists in private practice.

* Programming development for adults in professional and business markets is nearly endless, and can include corporate team building, leadership development, and skill building for groups or individuals. Just look to the outdoor adventure programs industry to see the parallels.

* Clients can also be built through straightforward self-referral, attracted to your program by your advertising program with radio, newspaper, or other means. This entails reaching individuals and families who might identify EAP and EAL as something that could help them. And then, of course, there are the both faith-based and secular programs produced to benefit churches, family agencies, and religious organizations.

This list is by no means inclusive. Brainstorm with others to determine other possible client populations for your program.

## Assessment Work as a Profit Center

**O**ne way to generate business requires having your staff therapists perform clinical assessment work on contract for outside organizations. For example, when a child enters the juvenile justice system in our area, the judge oftentimes orders a clinical assessment so that he or she can direct an appropriate treatment for the child. An outside organization is often contracted to perform both basic assessments or a whole battery of diagnostic testing that can include substance abuse screening. While this practice might not involve use of EAP or your horse partners, clinical assessment work is easily integrated into your therapists' schedules while bringing cash flow to the organization. In the process, your business builds awareness with the contracting organizations, families, and individual clients. Your program may also be the one ultimately recommended for and/or chosen by the individual in question.

## On-site Marketing

**G**etting people to understand who we are and what we do is a constant struggle in our business. And nothing is more effective at solving that problem and translating what we do than conducting on-site tours and demonstrations.

The difference between talking about what we do and experiencing what we do is similar to trying to describe an orange. I can spend all day describing what an orange tastes like, but until you bite into it, you will not truly know. Getting people out to the farm is the single best thing that can happen to your business. As a bonus, everyone who comes out to your farm becomes another advocate to help spread the word about your business.

There are three different ways we conduct on-site marketing at *Horse Sense*, and each targets a different audience: tours, demonstrations, and pro bono "seed" sessions.

* *Horse Sense* conducts free public tours 1-2 times a month. The tours are always on a Saturday from 10:30 to 11:30. Like a wide-angled lens, they bring in anybody . . . anybody and everybody . . . especially people who prefer to observe while still remaining somewhat anonymous. Tours give people the opportunity to find out who we are and what we do, get a feel for the place without having to call and make an appointment. We advertise the tours on our website, in the Activities/Calendar section of free local papers, the local women's magazine, and in the local pet-friendly magazine. Our free tour dates are listed in the local community calendars of area newspapers, radio stations, and TV.

* In contrast, our demonstrations are more focused, and done by invitation only to local licensed mental health professionals and other groups of specific targeting. During the demonstration, we have the audience participate in a specific exercise or introductory activity, followed by a physical tour of the facility and horses, and of course food and beverages. The demonstrations themselves are targeted specifically to the group involved, whether massage therapists, school administrators, counselors, or teachers. We end the demonstration with an evaluation form, which lets us get feedback from our guests. We promote these demonstrations through local mental health and therapist organizations; area school administrators, counselors, and teachers; and other health groups such as massage therapists, chiropractors, and alternative health organizations.

    *Horse Sense* also holds another set of demos for the professional business community and targeted corporations. Training managers or training directors are the most ideal contacts here; Human Resources managers are the appropriate contact if no training department exists. We hold these demonstrations either monthly or bimonthly, and offer two three-hour sessions throughout the day to accommodate busy schedules. You can sometimes find listings of HR directors and key corporate personnel in business magazines and business directories in your state. Individual company websites often yield names and contact information as well.

A key component to these and any demonstrations we offer is to provide some sort of evaluation at the end of the session. It is critical to get feedback from these professionals to gauge how well you did, determine what kind of information may be lacking, and to provide contact information for your database. Remember, these are people who will be crucial in referring business to your organization, so professionalism is important in every respect, from cleanliness of your facility to personal dress to language and presentation skills.

Both our tours and demonstrations are free. *Horse Sense* is still at a point where we do not want to cut off people who might become potential clients or referral sources. Deciding whether or not to charge for these functions is an issue being debated by many people in the field, and is entirely your own decision.

✳ The last type of onsite marketing is pro bono "seed" sessions designed to give potential clients a taste for the effectiveness of EAP or EAL for their organization. In the early days, we did up to ten pro bono sessions for a single school, only to have them back away due to lack of funding. Other organizations, however, have responded to our seed sessions with semester-long contracts for services.

Pro bono work does not guarantee that wonderful things will happen but they have been valuable nonetheless, helping to create awareness and getting a broad range of key market segments more familiar with who we are and what we do. I would suggest reserving pro bono sessions for key clients, and keeping the number of sessions down to a minimum. The idea is to give them a taste for the benefits you offer through your therapy . . . without giving away the farm.

## Grants: A Source of Funding, A Source of Clients

**I've already relayed the story of how *Horse Sense* was able to serve clients by accessing grant money in partnership with a local non-profit.** The collaboration we worked out helped both programs to expand clientele and services. But it

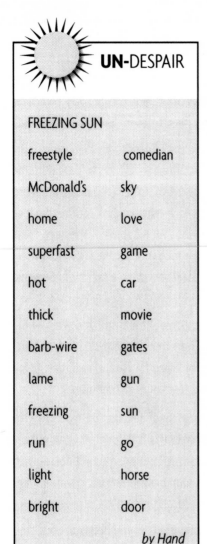

## UN-DESPAIR

**FREEZING SUN**

| | |
|---|---|
| freestyle | comedian |
| McDonald's | sky |
| home | love |
| superfast | game |
| hot | car |
| thick | movie |
| barb-wire | gates |
| lame | gun |
| freezing | sun |
| run | go |
| light | horse |
| bright | door |

*by Hand*

also helped a client population who would otherwise not have had access to our services without assistance.

The fun part of the story lies in how we managed to secure the grant despite how clueless we were at that time. It's a great illustration of how the impossible becomes possible when you have the enthusiasm, sincerity, and drive to make it happen. Necessity became the mother of invention, and inspired us to create an innovative solution that was a win-win for everybody.

On the flip side, the pursuit of grant funding is serious business, and should not be overlooked in the development of your program. *Horse Sense* now has various contractual arrangements for different programs and services. Not every grant requires non-profit status. However, our partnership with other non-profits—which extends beyond grant writing to joint fundraising and other efforts—has a synergistic effect on our shared mission, on manpower, time, and available programs. Whether your program is a for-profit or non-profit organization, the opportunity to collaborate brings greater good to your community.

Having grant money gives us the ability to reach out to organizations that might otherwise be closed to us. As an example, if we receive a large grant to treat at-risk youth from a community foundation, we're now in a position to call organizations like the area YWCA or YMCA and invite them up to our program. Even after the grant program is over, our relationship has now begun, and the door open for future collaboration and business.

Don't let anyone discourage you from trying this venue; *Horse Sense* had several people discourage us from even attempting our first grant. If you don't even try, you certainly won't ever know what can be possible. You should also know that it's possible to write a grant for a program and find the clients to fill it afterwards.

Use creative thinking for your fundraising efforts, too. *Horse Sense* raises money to develop a scholarship fund, which we then use to underwrite services to clients from local organizations or for clients without any resources. When you can combine grant funding (yours or theirs) with matched funds from a scholarship, you can suddenly make your services very affordable to organizations that might not otherwise be able to use you. We can match funds that they might spend by using our scholarship funds.

One of the best places to find sources of grant funding in your community is your local library. Many libraries have a nonprofit resource center with an enormous amount of material available on programs with available grants suitable for your organization. "Access Philanthropy" is another organization, based out of Minnesota, that specializes in finding sources of funding through corporate philanthropy, family trusts, and foundations. Access Philanthropy focuses on the giving preferences of these funding sources, and works with both for-profit and non-profit organizations who want to make better use of their limited research, marketing, and grant-seeking budgets. Find them through www.accessphilanthropy.com. You can hire Access Philanthropy on a consultation basis or simply access their database and website material for a fee. It's a wonderful resource to have at your fingertips, and has helped *Horse Sense* find many of the grants we've pursued.

Internet lists, like www.grants.gov, publish information about grants that are available in the community. You may want to subscribe to these to find grants suitable for your organization. The National Institute of Mental Health and many others have sections on their websites devoted to upcoming grants. You can also consult www.foundationcenter.org, a website that offers online trainings as well as keeping you informed about funding trends, available grants and other important information for funding your organization.

# The Art and Challenge of Writing Grants

**M**ake no mistake, grant writing is big business. Its sophistication has reached the point that many people make their living as professional researchers and grant writers. It can be intimidating to go up against organizations using professional grant writers; you may be tempted to throw in the towel without even trying.

Grant writing requires learning to think and write within an exact framework, and learning how to position your organization very specifically. In addition, each grant may have its writing requirements particular to the occasion. I strongly recommend finding grant-writing classes, either online or through your local community college. Learning the language of grant writing and developing a system will be important. Another resource is the *Grant Writing for Dummies* book by Beverly A. Browning. Like other books in the *Dummies* series, this book provides good, straightforward information for those learning how to write a grant on the fly.

Many funding organizations, like our local community foundation, have their own training seminar to teach applicants what they need to know for writing their grant. Some organizations don't even allow you to submit a grant without attending their grant writing class, a tactic designed to save pain, time, and effort on everyone's part. If the grant funding organization offers this type of class for submitting its grants, by all means be sure to attend.

On certain occasions, local colleges might have students who need a writing project for their major. Other organizations have been "adopted" by college classes, who then write the grant as a class project. If you actually go this route, know that the flip side may be a finished product that is less than stellar professionally. Be sure to create time to polish and review prior to the grant deadline.

Some organizations have an intermediate process to actually writing the grant itself, in which they require the applicant to submit a preliminary letter of intent that provides a brief sketch of the grant they intend to write. The funding organization will use this process to qualify applicants or to clarify the grant parameters. Either way, this step can save both organizations a lot of time and money should you be on the wrong track.

Once you have the basic grant template down, with language, references, and formats that work, all you will have to do is transfer the template from grant to grant, filling out anything specific to each situation.

Finally, don't wait until the last minute to learn how to write a grant. I can guarantee you'll barely have enough time to create the grant, much less learn as you go!

## Therapists and **Your Client Community**

**Y**our employees are your best customers . . . and like any other form of customer, they can do either a great deal of harm or a great deal of good as **ambassadors** of your organization. Before we close out this chapter from a "building clientele" perspective, I want to reiterate a point made earlier in the book: having therapists who are well-known within the mental health community can be a huge asset to your organization. Their professional relationships alone can represent an enormous return on investment that cannot be overestimated.

Think about it. Assuming that you are interested in offering Equine Assisted Psychotherapy, a large share of your business will come from the therapeutic community. You will have a much better chance being successful if that community can reference you based on who you have on staff. It's already strange enough to introduce EAP into the therapeutic community. It's tremendously helpful in terms of credibility if your therapist is someone they already know and respect.

Our therapists, Rob Jacoby and Laura Anthony, are perfect examples of this dynamic in action for *Horse Sense*. Prior to coming to *Horse Sense*, Laura had spent several years in various locations for a prominent community mental health organization here in North Carolina, and in the juvenile justice system in Florida prior to that. When she came over to *Horse Sense*, her enormous credibility in the community opened many doors that had previously been closed. Her credibility became our credibility.

Rob Jacoby had an extensive resume, with experience running a local drug treatment center, work with DUI and domestic violence groups for another mental health organization, work for the youth development center, and work with juvenile justice kids. His relationships in these circles helped us expand our access to the juvenile justice and youth development arenas. It led to getting part of a two-year $50,000 gang violence prevention grant to work with at-risk youth, among other opportunities. Be sure not to overlook this aspect when you think about your organization's marketing and client-building needs.

## Recommended **Reading**

*Attracting Perfect Customers*, Stacy Hall & Jan Brogniez

*Equinomics: the Secret to Making Money with Your Horse Business*, Lanier Cordell

*Grant Writing for Dummies*, Beverly A. Browning

www.accessphilanthropy.com

www.foundationcenter.org

www.grants.gov

Chapter **EIGHT**

## What Lies **Beyond:** MY **STORY** continued

*T**his past year has been the most successful year ever for** Horse Sense. We have a full slate of clients, two full-time therapist/ES teams, and one part-time. The team as a whole is dedicated, hard-working, and at the top of their game.*

*It's also been a year of looking in the mirror and seeing hard truths. These hard truths have prompted me to stretch and grow, to look at mistakes and learn how to do better. I feel like I'm breaking ground in every possible territory, both personally and professionally. Sometimes that's an invigorating feeling; sometimes it's a bit scary!*

*This past year we've performed our first strategic planning session, and came out the other side with new-found clarity for our future. I've been refining every aspect of our business, developing a Virtual Team of powerful professionals to help elevate my skills for everything from systems, management, finance, marketing, and networking.*

*I just wish I had done it sooner. If I had begun "with the end in mind," I would have planned with more care, spent with more thought, and paced our growth. On the other hand, I also realize there is a balance between planning and putting your business into a straightjacket. I realize that every business needs to have some "fly by the seat of your pants" aspects that are allowed to follow wherever the road may lead. You have to be knowledgeable and clear-headed, alert to the environment around you, yet nimble enough to adjust for the surprises and unexpectedly good things that may come your way. That's what balance is all about.*

So you've done your strategic plan, horses are cavorting in your pasture, the staff is up and running. Now the real work begins! As your journey into business ownership moves forward, you just might want to keep your eye on some of the paths ahead. This last chapter is a glimpse of what might be in store for you.

# Out of Infancy, Into Adolescence

**T**his book has been primarily about what we call the infancy stage, the very beginning of getting an equine assisted business up during the startup phase. We've tried to write about it while assuming nothing . . . because there was not a whole lot to assume about *me* when I started this adventure several years ago! We want to give each reader a good overview of what to expect, what choices to make, and what pitfalls to avoid. However, once you emerge from the infancy stage and start moving into adolescence, you will find yet another set of opportunities, challenges, and choices awaiting. That's what our second *Horse Sense, Business Sense* book will be about.

How do you know when you've reached the adolescent stage of your business? Here's a few indications:

✱ You achieve a steady stream of clients, and a relatively full schedule. The good news is that there's a demand for your business. Now you have to make sure it's a healthy demand. Whether these are good clients, or *productive* clients for your business becomes the question. At *Horse Sense*, we came to realize the difference between the two when we were booked solid with a waiting list of people, but still had poor cash flow. What was wrong? We realized that we didn't have a good balance between Medicare, grants, contracts, and self-pay clients, which had a negative impact on our financial health.

✱ You begin to see some financial stability thanks to regular clients and regular income. Things might still be tight, but you're no longer scratching out a daily existence.

✱ You may begin to experience a concept called "busy-ness versus productivity." You will find yourself just as busy as can be at a certain point, unable to take on even one thing more. Examine this situation carefully; while you *may* be busy, you might not necessarily be productive. In your infancy, when things are slow and schedules a bit more relaxed, you can fudge on some of the details because you have time on your hands. When you reach adolescence, any wasteful spots in your systems and scheduling will become very clear.

# UN-DESPAIR

Dear Judge

My name is ⬤⬤⬤⬤⬤⬤⬤ ; I was committed to DJJDP in December of 2003. I have spent two years in the system. During this time I have had a lot of ups and downs. I am now in the stage of maturity. I have really decided to get my life in order. Spending time in the system has made me except responsibly for my actions. I have had a lot of thinking errors I wanted to blame other for my reactions. I thought that having my friend was more important. But sitting alone in my room at night I know that my life is my own responsibly. And realizing it's just me. I am the person that can change me. I now understand what empathy really means. In this life I can not continue to hurt others without knowing that I'm hurting myself. I would not have admitted this two years ago. But as time goes, I would like to go also. I would like to finely be a teenager. I wont to do a lot of things normal kids my age do. I'm now in a program call I.D.P. For 13 months, This program is a 5 month long. I spent 8 more months trying to figure out discipline. This program helps people like me keep anger management. Well its has taken me more time than I wont to admit that , I couldn't get it together, I continue to not except or acknowledge my criminal behavior. I've had chances and chances. But my wake up call was when I started a program call horse sense. This program takes you out of the facility, into the community and on a horse farm. I was so amazed when I first entered the farm. I was at peace, I felt so much happiness when I was outdoors. I know that I am ready to have a-chance of improving myself. I wont to give more and I wont to be independent. I would like to go to Independent Living. Independent living will give me the skills I need in life. I thank God that I'm getting a second chance. I know that I will have to make good decisions at this home. I would like this to be an opportunity that would be good and positive for me. I'm learning new skills now like caring and loving others and myself, that is a beginning for me that I plan to continue all my life.

A letter written to the judge from one of our clients from the Swannanoa Valley Youth Development Center, a juvenile detention facility which is effectively the last chance for rehabilitation before youth are introduced into the adult prison system.

✱ You may realize you're reaching the outer limits of your expertise, or a point where your weakness in certain areas of business may become more apparent. You know that to continue operating in this mode will no longer work for your long-term viability. You realize you need help from the outside.

This can occur in several different areas. Maybe the bookkeeping is now over your head, or the tax filing too complicated. Or perhaps you know you need deeper management skills. Maybe you need to buy media for your advertising, but realize the process is too complicated without some expertise. When I reached this stage, I realized my business would no longer work the way I knew how to operate. And ultimately, if I didn't change, we as a business were not going to be around for long.

The best thing I did was start working with a professional business coach to elevate my business skills to a more sophisticated level. The process gave me a chance to step back and get perspective, identify the problem areas, and develop the skills I was missing. It then helped me to identify where I needed to outsource specific professional services, like marketing and finance. I strongly recommend you consider business coaching, preferably before you reach this stage. That way you can be ready, and ready to move fast, when the need arrives.

✱ You reach a point where you absolutely, positively cannot do it yourself any more. You cannot learn everything you need to learn, implement things, and see clients on a daily basis. You need to develop your team to include other functions for the business, like adding an administrative assistant, a receptionist, a bookkeeper, or an office manager. Somebody has to take this load so that you don't become a quasi-receptionist instead of the person who manages the business. If you haven't before, this is the time to start tracking how much time you actually spend working in your business as an ES or as a therapist, instead of working on your business. When your time is getting constrained because you're trying to do everything single-handedly, it's time to stop.

Adolescence is a time of both positive growth and profound change for both you and your program. Personally, I've seen significant differences in myself since the day we opened. My DiSC® personality profile pegs me as a natural "Steady" personality, not a natural leader. I've had to modify and develop my leadership skills in the office. I've really come to understand what the concepts of management, networking, and marketing really mean versus what I thought they meant in the beginning. At the same time, I can also say that I continue to feel the effects of my early mistakes, hoping that they were not so big that they overcome us.

In adolescence, marketing needs will become more sophisticated. Instead of using the simplified process outlined in earlier chapters, you may need to actually use a marketing consultant with some strategic planning, production, and media buying expertise. As you broaden your reach and impact in the community, you must reflect the more mature status of a growing company. That homemade logo or simplistic website that makes you look like a start-up will no longer do.

You may start suffering from the consequences of weak marketing from your early years (as we are now). You will have to make up for gaps in miscommunication or gaps in credibility due to an incomplete and incorrect public image. You may have to spend extra time or money making up ground, right about the time when you need to draw significantly more clients to support your growing staff.

Tracking and systems continue to be important for the growing business. You might need to consider a telephone system that won't give customers a busy signal, a data line for faxes, and software for scheduling and processing clients.

The need for information will become more sophisticated. You'll need to standardize tracking for number of client contact hours, staff productivity, clients by demographic and type. If 70% of your business is Medicaid clients, the other 30% will not be able to make up the difference that you need to stay afloat, so maintaining certain client ratios becomes important. Tracking statistical data on both your programs and client populations are important for:

* determining key marketing decisions,

* presenting the latest statistics when making presentations to professionals and referral sources,

* submitting to the industry as a whole as part of our global statistics tracking, and

* tracking progress on your strategic goals and objectives to measure success during the year.

## Team Concerns

**I**n adolescence, you should see the money you've invested in training and developing your team begin to pay off. Now you have to maintain and administer to the team needs. At the same time, as schedules get tight and communication less relaxed, weaknesses in your team development may begin to show. Be prepared to support your team's continued growth and confidence as they find their footing in your program.

Another aspect to remember about your team is that by doing this intense EAP and EAL work, close friendships between you and your staff are bound to develop beyond the work itself. I find myself becoming friends with virtually every coworker on staff, if we weren't friends beforehand. It requires special skills to negotiate the duality of relationships on a close team. Pay special attention to introducing new staff to your team. If you've developed an especially "tight" core team that's survived the ups and downs of your program's infancy, a new person may have an especially hard time breaking in.

At *Horse Sense*, that has meant developing more standardized protocols to circumvent a build up of issues, including session debriefings and conflict resolution. Not only do you need to know if you are on target and if sessions are going in a good direction, but you need to have a plan in place should internal difficulties and disagreements arise. It is delicate, hard work that we do. Trust and tight communication with each other are critical.

In order to provide continuity of care for the client, continuity between different team members becomes pretty important, and communication between the team members becomes more important as the staff grows. Of course, more staff also equals more cooks in the kitchen, so scheduling and office flow is going to become important. More training is indicated for policies like HIPPA.

Maintaining a staff is going to take more of your time and thought as your business grows. More people also increase pressure on payroll and overhead, which then trickles down into cash flow. Programs with significant insurance or contract billing will have to negotiate the tricky ground of delayed payment for services. A benefits program becomes a reality for those who haven't implemented one earlier, including things like vacation and sick pay, health insurance, and workman's compensation. Management responsibilities increase as daily staff needs and concerns come into play. You will have to manage training programs, meet professional protocols, hire and fire, and manage nondiscrimination policies.

An office manager or receptionist becomes a pretty high priority once you start stepping into that next level. A receptionist will answer phones and be the first point of contact for your business. And if you have multiple treatment teams going at one time, an office manager will run the team, check clients in and out, be in charge of scheduling, and handle billing and collections. Experience in running a small medical practice would be ideal, though not always affordable.

## Beyond Adolescence to "Established"

**H**ow do you know when your business is firmly established and past all the worries and concerns of infancy and adolescence? Probably never! However, depending on who you ask, there are some "soft" benchmarks that might give you a clue that your program has reached a more comfortable and established cycle in its life. Here's some definitions provided by different business professionals:

The Chief Financial Officer (CFO) of a company might say you've reached the established stage when you have a consistent, positive cash flow over and above the operations of the business. In other words, you can pay your bills, make payroll, and always have money in the bank, enough to pay every bill in Accounts Payable no matter when it falls in your cash cycle. The percentage of cash above expenses depends on your business. It may be 10% for some, 5% for others.

A banker would say you've reached maturity when you've met their formulas and cash-to-debt ratios. A simple ratio in this regard would be 20% cash to debt service payment. So if you have a monthly payment of $10,000 on your business debt, you would need $2,000 in cash, *above and beyond payroll and monthly expenses* to make this ratio. A banker would also say an established business needs assets, things like land and equipment. However, if you've set up your business like *Horse Sense*, assets are leased from another business entity. If that's the case, your leasing entity is the one holding the hard assets, and your leasing entity would need to be the business securing the loan.

A marketing professional would say your business has become established when you have a sufficient flow of productive (as in paying) customers to meet your income goals. The customer flow is such that you only need a "maintenance" advertising and marketing program, one based on increasing sales incrementally vs. drawing the base platform of customers.

Know that even when you get to the established stage, you will have new and more sophisticated challenges. You may find that, having reached this stage, you no longer like running your business or doing what you're doing. You might want to hand your business over to a management team so that you can go back to working with the horses or having more client contact. Or you may want to sell your business and try something else. Neither of these options are wrong; they just need to be planned. It's your job to keep in touch with your inner vision, and then make the changes necessary to renew or honor that vision.

In the established stage, annual strategic planning will become even more important. As your team grows and the business becomes more complex, keeping all the moving parts in alignment is only accomplished through a strategic process that involves the entire team and brings people back to the same page. No matter how professional your staff, how well you each know your business, or how smoothly things run, the pieces start falling out of place in minute increments that are easy to miss. Those increments build up to major cracks over time, and can really derail things if you don't have a process that mines and repairs them on a regular basis. Strategic planning does that.

You also need strategic planning because the marketplace never, ever remains static. Part of the strategic planning process involves scanning the marketplace, observing trends from the past year, researching movement in the present, and then looking into the year ahead. What shifts are about to happen? How are global, national, and regional events in the economy, in politics, and in the social environment going to trickle down to impact you? For this purpose, strategic planning is a lot like playing tennis. You hit the ball over the net, and observe how the other player reacts. You notice how he positions his next shot, then *set your stance* to best return the volley. And while you can't predict exactly what will transpire, you can set yourself up to the most advantageous position. That, too, is strategic planning.

In 2006, the mental health services landscape in our region shifted dramatically, with one major mental health organization imploding and a juvenile justice facility in danger of closing. Both organizations were responsible for serving significant portions of the population, and both impacted our business. We used our strategic planning to understand and identify the opportunities these shifts created for us while also trying to understand the lessons and challenges they represented. Again, setting our stance . . . being ready.

## MY **STORY** to be continued

*A friend of mine once said, "We can plan for tomorrow but we can't plan tomorrow's outcomes." We can never know what the future will bring, but then again, that's not our job. We are in charge of doing the footwork, the planning, and the preparation needed for tomorrow. The rest really is not up to us.*

*I think it's important not to compare yourself to the "perfect program." We've all heard about the program where someone wrote a huge grant and got their entire business up and running in one fell swoop. Or, maybe they barely open their doors and are loaded with clients overnight. While it does happen, know that sometimes our path is a little more challenging. It's okay to take a little longer to get there. I encourage you to plan well, get professional support, and set sound benchmarks for your organization. Then use those benchmarks as opportunities to measure yourself and chart your own form of success.*

*I am delighted to see the number of people who are coming into equine assisted practice with business savvy. But if your "Business Sense" could use more work, I encourage you to use the resources in this book and elsewhere to educate yourself. I originally equated the cold, calculating world of Corporate America with small business, but it's a totally different universe. Are there sharks in suits everywhere? Absolutely. But there's also really wonderful people you want to know, work, and play with!*

*Whether we are for-profit or non-profit businesses, we all need to be strong as entrepreneurs. It is my hope that this book has served to help you on the road to your own successful equine assisted practice. Know that there are problems, worry, and anxiety . . . but also growth, fulfillment, and tremendous learning ahead for you. We are fortunate to be part of this amazing field. We're doing wonderful work that's a positive force in the world. Armed with dedication, and knowledge, we can help each other reach new heights. I can't wait to see what Horse Sense does next. And I can't wait to see what all of you do next!*

# Works Cited and Recommended Reading

### Equine Assisted Practices

*Adventures in Awareness*, Barbara Rector

*Equine Assisted Psychotherapy Business Planning Guide & Workbook*, Barbara J. Scott

*Equine Facilitated Mental Health: A Field Guide*, by Boo McDaniel

*Horses Don't Lie*, Chris Irwin

*Horse Sense & Human Heart*, Adele and Deborah McCormick

*Horse Sense for the Leader Within*, Arianna Strozzi

*Introduction to Equine-Assisted Psychotherapy*, Patti J. Mandrell

*It's Not About the Horse*, Wyatt Webb

*Riding Between the Worlds*, Linda Kohanov

*Tao of Equus*, Linda Kohanov

www.eagala.org

www.egea.org

www.mnlinc.org

www.narha.org

www.naropa.edu

www.okcorralseries.com

www.prescott.edu

www.taoofequus.com

### Business

*4 Obsessions of an Extraordinary Executive*, Patrick Lencioni

*5 Dysfunctions of a Team*, Patrick Lencioni

*E-Myth Revisited*, Michael Gerber

*E-Myth Physician*, Michael Gerber

*Good to Great*, Jim Collins

*Non-Profit for Dummies*, Stan Hutton and Frances Phillips

*The One Page Business Plan*, Jim Horan

*Owner's Manual for Small Business*, Rhonda Abrams

*The 7 Habits of Highly Effective People*, Stephen Covey

*Small Business for Dummies*, Eric Tyson and Jim Schell

www.smallbusinessschool.org

## Funding

www.AngelsCapitalAssociation.org

www.accessphilanthropy.com

www.grants.gov

www.onlinewbc.gov

www.sba.org

www.sba.gov/gopher/Local-Information/Certified-Preferred-Lenders

www.sba.gov/INV

www.sba.gov/sbdc

www.smallbusinessschool.com

www.score.org

## Marketing and Grantwriting

*Attracting Perfect Customers*, Stacy Hall & Jan Brogniez

*Equinomics: the Secret to Making Money with Your Horse Business*, Lanier Cordell

*Grant Writing for Dummies*, Beverly A. Browning

*Guerrilla Marketing: Secrets for Making Big Profit from Your Small Business*,
Jay Conrad Levinson

*How to Make a Living Without a Job*, Barbara Winter

*Marketing Makeover Kit*, Kendall Summerhawk

*Money, Meaning & Beyond*, Andrea Lee

*Small Business Marketing for Dummies*, Barbara Findlay Schenck


**Horses/Animals in General**

*Animals in Translation*, Temple Grandin

*Cesar's Way*, Cesar Millan

*Horse Behavior & Psychology DVD Program*, Parelli

*Horsekeeping on a Small Acreage: Designing and Managing Your Equine Facility*, Cherry Hill

*Natural Horse Care*, Pat Coleby

*Natural Horse-Man-Ship*, Pat Parelli

Parelli Level 1 Theory & Psychology

*Revolution in Horsemanship*, Dr. Robert Miller

*Stablekeeping: A Visual Guide to Safe and Healthy Horsekeeping*, Cherry Hill

*Thinking in Pictures*, Temple Grandin

*Understanding the Ancient Secrets of the Horse's Mind*, Dr. Robert Miller


**Other Good Books (not mentioned elsewhere)**

*Emotional Intelligence*, Daniel Goleman

*Fierce Conversations*, Susan Scott

*Move Closer, Stay Longer*, Stephanie Burns

*Waking the Tiger*, Peter Levine

## Acknowledgements

I've been so blessed in the writing of this book to have enormous help and inspiration from many people and horses. First I'd like to thank Brenda Dammann, a wonderful co-writer and partner through this process. It could **not** have happened without you, and I am grateful for your dedication and determination to see this through. Your assistance and guidance was crucial to our success! I'd also like to thank Ginger Graziano and Lauri Bayless for their Herculean efforts and their roles in getting this book finished and looking great! Thank you too, Coco Baptist, for your inspiring photographic work and your kind, smiling soul. Elizabeth Barbour, my life and business coach, has been a rock of support and my biggest fan as I have worked to improve *Horse Sense* and my life in relationship to it; she is truly an inspired and inspiring entrepreneur. Thanks also to Mark Lytle, my EAGALA supervisor and friend, whose seed of an idea became this book. Many, many thanks to all who helped make this a reality.

I would also like to thank those in the EAP/EAL field who have taught me and accompanied me along the way, including, in the early years, Mary Lynn Szymandera, Josie Saxton, and Lynn Clifford, and more recently Lynn Thomas, Mark Lytle, StarrLee Heady, David Currie, Mickie DiGiacomo, Mary Ayers, and Patti & Randy Mandrell. I have had the privilege of learning from each of you, and am honored to have done so. To my friends and co-workers at *Horse Sense*, past and present, I offer gratitude and thanks for putting up with me! Rob Jacoby, Laura Anthony, and Kacey Cramer, what else can I say but you're the **best**! Truly I'm honored and lucky to come to work every day with you three. So sayeth the donkey. Thanks and much love also goes to Lisa Wheeler, Meghan Flynn, and Valerie Krall.

I would further like to thank Pat and Linda Parelli, for their dedication to horses and humans and for their wonderful programs and courses of study. Thanks for putting in the perspiration and for sharing the knowledge with all of us, and for continuing to be an inspiration. Both Linda and Kaffa Martignier continue to inspire me with their horsemanship, their teaching skills and with their general life wisdom. My admiration for you both grows with each opportunity I have to work with you. I would also like to thank all the instructors and faculty whom I've studied with through the years: David Lichman, Carol Coppinger, Katja Taureg, Kelly Sigler, Helen Topp, Alain Martignier, Jesse Peters, Jerry Williams, Rachel & Don Jessop, and anyone else I've forgotten! You have all challenged me and demonstrated top teaching and people skills. Most of all I'd like to thank Ellen Hearne, for her passive persistence in the proper position, which finally got me to attend a Parelli event. As they say, "Contempt prior to investigation." Thanks for pushing me out of my comfort zone!

Last but certainly not least I wish to thank my brother Jamie Sikes, my mom Chris Sikes, and my dad Jimmie Sikes for the love, support, and encouragement freely given me throughout my life, and my husband, Richard, and our amazing horses. Richard, your humor, your hard work, and your determination are an inspiration to me, and I could never be doing what I'm doing without you by my side. All my love to you as we "trudge the road of happy destiny" together. To Dreamer, my sweet Palomino, and Sue, aka "Miss Piggy," I continually strive to be worthy of your trust and love, and your belief that I can be the person you need and want me to be. To Cody, Masada, Gus, Summer, Hook, and the rest of the herd, your capacity for forgiveness astounds me, as does your patience and kindness with us two-legged beings. To Snowball & Misty, thanks for taking care of me when I was young and horse crazy, and thanks most of all to Brandy, for telling me that which I could hear from no-one else. I am forever grateful to you. Finally, thank you to Lucky & Sugar, who did make it, and to Shadow & Dolly, who are now free, and to all the "rescue" horses I've had the honor of meeting through my life, for allowing me to be a part of yours. God, grant me the serenity to accept the things I cannot change, the courage to change the things I can, and the wisdom to know the difference. So be it.

# Index

Advertising, 119–20 *see also Marketing*

Alcoholics Anonymous, 29

Animal assisted therapy

    cutting edge professional field, as, 6

    techniques, 6

Anthony, Laura, 129

Anthropomorphism, 97

Barns

    rehab, 64

    rules for, 68

Branding, 116–17

Budgeting

    expenses *see Expenses*

    income *see Income*

    process, 40–1

Building and development, 62–5

Business

    adolescence stage, moving to, 132–5

    building, 13–14

    C-Corp, 21

    capital, 17–19

    daily, systems for, 50–1

    entrepreneur, 14–15

    established stage, 137–8

    establishment of, 1

    for-profit vs. non-profit, 19–21

    forms, 51–3

    growing, 42

    in-patient vs. outpatient, 22

    infancy stage, 132

    Limited Liability Corporation, 21–2

    needs of, 61–2

    paperwork, 51–3

    partnership, 21–2

    plan, 35–6

    S-Corp, 21–2

    sole proprietorship, 21

    start-up resources, 18

    structure, 19–22

    system, building, 34

    technician, 14–15

    Virtual Team, building, 16–17

    work, getting done, 15

    zoning issues, 36–7

Capital

    bootstrapping, 18

    business, funding, 17–19

    community organizations, from, 19

Cave diving facilities, 40

Celente, Gerald, 12

Clientele, building, 118–20

Clients, finding, 121–3

Clifford, Lynn, 10

Clinical assessments, 123

Comer, Candace, 6

Compensation, 45–7

Development, considerations, 62–5, 67

E-Myth, The, 14–15

Employees see Staff

Entrepreneur, becoming, 12–13

Epona Equestrian Services, 5

    Equine Facilitated Experiental Learning, 24

    foundation, 24

    workshops, 24

Equine assisted business

    building, 13–14

    choice and decisions, 11–12

    reasons for not starting, 13

    reasons for starting, 13

Equine Assisted Growth and Learning Association (EAGALA), 5

    foundation, 23

    mentoring supervision, 87

    model, use of, 25–6

    nature of, 23–4

    tenets, 24

    therapist, model for, 92–4

    training, 10

Equine Assisted Learning (EAL)

    advent of, 1

    Horse Sense of the Carolinas, Inc., business of, 2

    leading organizations, 5

    moving parts in business, 3

    team, hiring, 78–80

    training, horses for, 72–6

Equine Assisted Personal Development (EAPD), 25

Equine assisted practice

    disciplines and schools, 25

    equine specialist, 95 see also Equine specialist

    explaining, 118

    horses with issues, 71–2

    in-patient vs. outpatient, 22

    mental and emotional exercise, 77

    natural horsemanship, marriage with, 99–100

    other therapeutic practices compared, 5

    pasture, activity in, 62

    props, 61

    scheduling, 57

    structures for, 58–9

    team, working as, 86–9

    team-based structure, 70–1

    theoretical models of, 22

    trading out therapy, 94–5

    types of programs, 22

    value of, 1

Equine assisted program

    perfect, 139

    principles and models, 32

Equine Assisted Psychotherapy (EAP)

    advent of, 1

    client community, 129

clients, finding, 121–3

delivery of services, 93

experiental setting, 110

*Horse Sense of the Carolinas, Inc.*, business of, 2

leading organizations, 5

moving parts in business, 3

self-report, 90

team, hiring, 78–80

therapist, world of, 89–94

traditional models of psychotherapy, differing from, 89

training, horses for, 72–6

Equine assisted therapy

mental health therapists, by, 6

pitfalls, 7

Equine Facilitated Mental Health Association (EFMHA), 5

practices, 24

Equine Guided Education Association, 25

Equine specialist

attributes, 95–9

good, finding, 83

role of, 95

scheduling, 57

special interests, 55

student of horses, as, 96

therapist, not, 99

trouble spots, 95–9

Equine therapy

facility, handling, 30–1

international programs, 11

Expenses

categories of, 47

facility, of, 49

general, 48–50

income, calibration against, 49

program costs and expenditures, 47

shopping around, 50

staff, of, 49

Facility

building, 61

buildings, 62–5

development, considerations, 67

equine assisted activity, for, 58–9

expenses, 49

indoor arena, 64–6

pasture, 61

rehab barns, 64

rental, 30–1

rules for, 68

structures, 62–5

usable land, 58

Fencing, 67

Forms, crucial, 51–3

Fundraising, 127

Gang Violence Prevention Program, 126

Gerber, Michael, 14

Grant writing, 128

Grants, 44–5, 125–7

Head, Heart, Hands & Horses program, 2
*Horse Sense of the Carolinas, Inc.*, 2
  building, 10–11
  business system, building, 34
  EAGALA model, adoption of, 25–6
  Guiding Principles, 88–9
  handling model, 27–8
  non-mounted therapy, as, 26–7
  opening, 9
  team, guiding philosophy, 29
  therapist job description, 94
Horses
  anthropomorphism, 97
  burnout, 76–7
  care and nutrition, 60
  disassociated state, in, 74–5
  handling, 27–8
  issues, with, 71–2
  jobs with, 6
  landing period, 74
  means to an end, as, 97–8
  mental and emotional exercise, 77
  other horses, needing, 60
  physical health, regaining, 74
  reaction, using, 32, 88
  rehabilitation, 75–6
  requirements of, 59–61
  rescue, 71–2

  training, 72–6
  unrideable, homes for, 9
Human resources
  function of, 54
  standard procedures, 54–5

Income
  general, 41–2
  grant money, 44–5, 125–7
  rates, setting, 42–3
  sliding scale fees, 43–4
Indoor arena, 64–6
  rules for, 68
Insurance
  billing, 45–7
  claims processing, 46
  health, 54, 79
  paperwork, 45–6
  professional liability, 39–40
  program and farm, for, 38–9
Irwin, Chris, 25

Jacoby, Rob, 89–94, 129

Kersten, Greg, 25

Liability
  issues, 38–9
  professional, 39–40
  program and farm, 38–9

Lytle, Mark, 2

Market, determining, 120–1

Marketing

 active, 112–14

 activities being, 103–4

 adolescence stage, in, 135

 advertising, 119–20

 attitude to, 101

 branding, 116–17

 concept, 119

 doing it right, 104

 features of business, focus on, 110

 finding out what market wants, 104–6

 grid, creating, 107–8

 implementing, 111–14

 information, provision of, 103

 mailing lit, 106

 materials, developing, 110–11

 message, development of, 109

 need for, 102–3

 on-site, 114, 123–5

 philosophy for, 102

 placements, 112

 plan, 103

 repeating, 116–17

 strategic planning, 107–8

 thinking process, 106

 tracking results, 114–16

Minnesota Linking Individuals, Nature and Critters (MNLINC), 25

Natural Horsemanship, 28–9

 equine assisted practices, and, 99–100

North American Riding for the Handicapped Association (NARHA), 5, 24

OK Corral, 25

Parelli horsemanship system, 28–9

 Friendly Game, 73

 mental and emotional exercise, 77

 Seven Games, 9

 use of, 8

Parelli, Pat, 3

Recommended Reading lists, 5

Rector, Barbara, 25

Safety

 contract, scope of, 53

 high-risk clients, 69

 issues, 54

 personnel, of, 69

Scheduling, 57

Small business statistics, 10–11

Staff

 cross-utilization, 79–80

 expenses, 49

 failure rate, 1

 feedback, 87

 friends, as, 82–3

health insurance, 54, 79

hiring procedures, 55

Honesty, Open-Mindedness and Willingness, 87

hour, paid by, 55

internships, 55–6

interviewing, 84–5

maintaining, 136

meetings, 56–7, 81–2

mental and emotional fitness, 85–6

non-compete agreement, 80–1

qualified, finding, 83

Standard Operating & Procedures manual, 51, 81

team, as, 86–9

team building, 70–1

team concerns, 136

team, hiring, 78–80

training, 79

vacations, 79

volunteers, 55–6

Standard Operating Procedures

attempt to create, 2

manual, 51, 81

Strategic planning, 107–8, 131, 138

Strozzi, Arianna, 25

Team

building, 70–1

concerns, 136

hiring, 78–80

staff as, 86–9

Technician business, 14–15

Un-Despair file, 4

Virtual Team, building, 16–17

Women at Risk, 118

Zoning issues, 36–7

# About the Authors

## Shannon Knapp

In the quiet hillsides outside of Asheville, NC, *Horse Sense of the Carolinas* has been nudging clients in a new direction.

Shannon Knapp received her Masters from the University of Florida in 1993, and spent many years teaching college English and literature. In 2000, she and her husband, Richard, a computer programmer in telecommunications, moved from Texas to Western North Carolina to pursue their dream of having their own farm and helping horses in need. Shannon is the founder and President of *Horse Sense*, an Equine Assisted Therapy and Learning Center which began as a result of working with abused & neglected horses.

Shannon has attended workshops with and studied many of the different schools of thought that comprise Equine Assisted Activities, including EAGALA, EFMHA, Epona, EGEA, AIA and EAHAE. She received her EAGALA Advanced Certification in late 2006, and has become sought out as a leader in this field, both in her understanding of Equine Assisted Psychotherapy and Equine Assisted Learning programs, but also in understanding the business side as well. As part of her consulting practice, she conducts onsite and offsite workshops, hosts teleclasses and offers one-on-one consultation with others like her who want to help create positive change in their community through working with horses.

Shannon started out to help horses and found a significant way to help people as well. Horses have been an important part of her personal journey, and she is honored and grateful to be able to share the horses with others through *Horse Sense*.

## Brenda Dammann

Brenda Dammann is a freelance writer whose extensive background includes experience in television production, marketing management, and theme park project management. Her skill in transforming complex creative and technical information into remarkable content has been a proven asset for her clients in a variety of capacities and multiple venues. She enjoys adapting to the unique and challenging situations each project provides. Brenda and her husband live outside Asheville, NC, where their own personal journey with two Paso Fino horses is underway. Find her at www.creativeinc.net.

Ready to **Make a Difference?**

*Horse Sense* offers a variety of resources that help you be successful in your EAP/EAL business. Visit our website for more information and details about how you can get extra support! Visit www.HorseSenseOtc.com and learn more about . . .

**Free Information, Free Telecalls, Free Reports, and More!**
• Our monthly newsletter, free monthly telecalls, our blog and other items, keeping you informed about key issues and exciting, important developments in the field

**Consultations**
• Individualized, 1 on 1 consultation, Consultation packages, and Project consultation programs to help you with specific goals

**Programs**
• Telecalls, Teleclasses, and Onsite Workshops, both day-long and multi-day events

**Products**
• Activity Guidebooks and Program Journals from existing *Horse Sense* groups. *Upcoming:* Audio CD's and CD packages on a range of topics to help you succeed, and Step-by-Step Workbook Companions to guide your way

Shannon is dedicated to the success of the field, and to your success as a provider of services. The more quality EAP/EAL programs, the more people know about our work, the more clients benefit, and the more we work together the improve the lives of horses and humans everywhere. We are not competitors! The more of us out there doing this, and most importantly doing it *well*, simply raises the profile of our profession, from which we all benefit.